A MESSIANIC PERSPECTIVE ON TITHING AND CHARITY

WHAT ABOUT TITHING?

TOBY JANICKI

WHAT ABOUT TITHING?

TOBY JANICKI

Printed in the United States of America

ISBN: 978-1-892124-82-1

Cover design: Joel Powell

Quantity discounts are available on bulk purchases of this book for educational, fundraising, or event purposes. Special versions or book excerpts to fit specific needs are available from First Fruits of Zion. For more information, contact www.ffoz.org/contact.

First Fruits of Zion

PO Box 649, Marshfield, Missouri 65706–0649 USA
Phone (417) 468–2741, www.ffoz.org

Comments and questions: www.ffoz.org/contact

Contents

Introduction

There is a lot of confusion about tithing among believers today. Are we required to tithe? Does the Torah obligate us to give 10 percent of our incomes? If so, to whom should we be tithing? At First Fruits of Zion, we get these kinds of questions about tithing all the time. It's one of the frequently asked questions we see most often.

Tithing is extensively discussed and explained in our *Torah Club: Unrolling the Scroll* and *Torah Club: Depths of the Torah*, but those discussions are scattered across the Torah Club volumes because they are offered as commentary on the specific commandments of tithing as they appear in the Torah. Tithing laws show up all throughout the Torah. This book brings all that Torah Club material together into one place and adds a lot of additional information.

In *What About Tithing* we will explore the background of tithing from the ancient Near East and the book of Genesis and take a detailed look at the complex tithing system as it is found in the Torah. We will also study the tithing theme as it appears in the Gospels, the Epistles, the book of Revelation, as well as in early Jewish-Christian literature.

Because it is important to our study of the laws of tithing, the overarching biblical themes of charity and generosity will be examined as well. Then we will combine the concepts with the practical application of the laws of tithing in our own lives today.

Tithing and giving are important topics in the life of a disciple of Yeshua and that's why First Fruits of Zion has dedicated an entire book to the subject. It is our hope that this will not only challenge the reader to reconsider their own tithing practice but also commit to a life of giving that we see so often exemplified by the great men of faith and taught by our Master Yeshua. May this book serve to draw us all closer to HaShem and strengthen our walk of discipleship.

1
The Origins of Tithing

It may come as a surprise to some to learn that tithing did not originate with the Bible, and neither is it an exclusively Israelite practice. Tithing is widely documented throughout the ancient Near East.

The Ancient Near East

Tithes in the ancient Near East were taken from property or from spoils of war and set aside for sacral use. Although the earliest documents attesting to tithing in Mesopotamia only go back to the sixth century BCE, the practice itself dates to a much earlier period.[1] The biblical text attests to the antiquity of tithing in non-Israelite nations, as in Genesis where we read that the Egyptians gave two tenths of their produce to Pharaoh.[2]

We have evidence from Syro-Palestine (which essentially covers northern Israel and Syria) of the practice of tithing dating back to the fourteenth century BCE—two centuries before the giving of the Torah.[3] The Syro-Palestinian tithes went not only to temples but also to kings, who would then distribute them to their officials. This overlap in the tithe's recipient existed because the ancient temples were often considered royal, as evidenced by biblical texts such as Amos 7:13—"Never again prophesy at Bethel, for it is the king's sanctuary, and it is a temple of the kingdom"—and Genesis 28, in which is mentioned the priest-king Melchizedek. The funds were then the king's to use at his discretion.

The first-century BCE Greek historian Diodorus described the annual offerings given by the Carthaginians (the inhabitants of a Phoenician city) to the temple of Melqart in Tyre:

> Since they had come as colonists from that city, it had
> been their custom in the earlier period to send to the
> god a tenth of all that was paid into the public revenue.
> (Diodorus, *Bibliotheca Historica* 20:14)

In Ugaritic documents and in Mesopotamia we find evidence of tithing on grain, beverages, and a wide array of goods such as agricultural crops, animals, cloth, and metal.[4] It also appears that in the ancient Near East the tithe was sometimes voluntary and other times obligatory. Thus, at times the tithe looked more like a tax than an offering.

From the evidence we learn that the tithes were stored in temples, and the temple representatives were placed in charge of them. Some of the funds went toward the upkeep of the temple and the attached facilities. Animal tithes would have been used for sacrifices and the agriculture tithes distributed to the priests and others for consumption.[5]

The fact that the practice of tithing is not exclusively an Israelite or biblical practice does not diminish the Torah's commandments on tithing but rather shows that tithing has been deeply ingrained in man from the beginning of time. It has always been a way for the individual to express thanks and gratitude for provision and protection received. The Torah merely dictates how followers of HaShem are to carry out the practice and gives details as to where the tithe is to go.

Abraham

We have two pre-Mosaic examples in the book of Genesis of the Patriarchs giving tithes. The first occurs when Abraham returned from rescuing his nephew Lot from the hands of the four empires that had attacked Sodom. He met a mysterious figure named Melchizedek, who accordingly is labeled both a king and a priest:

> Melchizedek king of Salem brought out bread and wine.
> (He was priest of God Most High.) And he blessed him.
> … And Abram gave him a tenth of everything. (Genesis
> 14:18–20)

The LORD has sworn and will not change his mind,
"You are a priest forever after the order of Melchizedek."
(Psalm 110:4)

Abraham gave Melchizedek (the priest-king) a tenth of everything, which the context seems to infer was a tenth of the spoils of war. This is in line with the ancient Near Eastern practices in which tithes were sometimes separated from the spoils of war and also given to a royal temple.

The Hebrew word for "tithe" here is *ma'aser* (מעשר), which literally means "a tenth part." Some commentators, such as Rashi, actually feel that Abraham, in tithing to Melchizedek, was fulfilling in advance the commandment to tithe that was later given in the Torah. While these same commentators are divided as to specifically which tithing commandment Abraham fulfilled, nevertheless a biblical principle of giving a 10-percent tithe in certain circumstances was established in his offering to Melchizedek.[6]

Abraham's practice of tithing also shows his generosity in stark contrast to the greed of the king of Sodom:

> The king of Sodom said to Abram, "Give me the persons, but take the goods for yourself." But Abram said to the king of Sodom, "I have lifted my hand to the LORD, God Most High, Possessor of heaven and earth, that I would not take a thread or a sandal strap or anything that is yours, lest you should say, 'I have made Abram rich.' I will take nothing but what the young men have eaten, and the share of the men who went with me. Let Aner, Eshcol, and Mamre take their share." (Genesis 14:21–24)

The Torah reveals a lot about the character of those whose lives are recorded in its pages by the first words they utter. The first phrase we hear from the king of Sodom is a short six-word declaration beginning with "Give me." This displays a characteristic of greed, which the Prophet Ezekiel later relates permeated the people of Sodom.[7] Abraham, on the other hand, gave a tithe of everything, showing us a clear example of his generous spirit. The Torah teaches that the giving of a tithe exposes in a person the opposite of the spirit of greed.

Jacob

Another example of tithing in Genesis is found in the story of Jacob in which he had just fled from his brother Esau. One night as he slept, Jacob had a dream about a ladder leading up to heaven. In the dream HaShem made promises to him about the blessings that his offspring would have. When he awoke, Jacob set up a pillar and declared,

> If God will be with me and will keep me in this way that I go, and will give me bread to eat and clothing to wear, so that I come again to my father's house in peace, then the LORD shall be my God, and this stone, which I have set up for a pillar, shall be God's house. And of all that you give me I will give a full tenth to you. (Genesis 28:20–22)

So once again we find a connection between ancient Near Eastern practices and that of the Torah. In the story of Jacob we have a temple connection in that he named the place of his dream *Beit El* ("House of God," בית־אל, Genesis 28:19), and we also have the declaration of tithing.

Jacob's words "I will give a tenth" literally reads from the Hebrew "tithe I shall, tithe." While Rabbi Hirsch translated this idiomatically as "repeatedly tithe," other rabbinic commentators are convinced that the repetition of the word "tithe" means that he promised to give 20 percent of all his possessions. This second interpretation would be more in line with the grain tithes in the Torah in which a tenth went to the Levites and a tenth to the poor, equaling around 20 percent. Whether Jacob's declaration means 10 or 20 percent, once again the principle of tithing was established.[8]

These tithing narratives lay the groundwork and establish principles that are later picked up on in the Torah and established as canon law. In the next chapter we will explore the main tithing system of the Torah.

2
The Tithing System of the Torah

The Torah's system of tithing is quite complex. There are numerous passages throughout the books of Exodus, Leviticus, Numbers, and Deuteronomy detailing tithing legislation. At a cursory glance it appears that these texts are unorganized and perhaps even contradictory at times.

This seeming chaos is so severe that it has caused many modern scholars to assume that these various tithing passages reflect different practices from different periods of Israelite history and have been artificially bunched together in the text of Torah. We will reject this assumption and instead examine the traditional Jewish interpretation, which groups the various tithing passages into one organized system.

Basic Principles

Before examining the Torah's laws in depth, we will need to establish a few basic principles. First, it is clear from the text of the Torah that tithing is applicable only to crops. For example, Deuteronomy 14:22 states: "You shall tithe all the yield of your seed that comes from the field year by year." The Torah is not talking about one's monetary income but specifically agricultural crops.

Second, not only are the tithes in the Torah applicable just to crops but specifically to crops grown in the land of Israel and not in the Diaspora. Additionally, most Jewish authorities rule that these tithes are only biblically required on grain (wheat, barley, oats, spelt, and rye), wine (grapes), and oil (olives).[9]

Finally, based upon "They shall not profane the holy things of the people of Israel, which they contribute to the LORD" (Leviticus 22:15), rabbinic tradition teaches that it is a violation of the Torah for an individual to consume un-tithed produce that was grown from any of these species in the land of Israel.[10]

It is also important to remember that the majority of the Torah's laws on tithing are not considered to be incumbent upon Gentiles.[11] These principles will be important to remember as we study the laws on tithing in the Torah and in the Apostolic Era.

Large Heave Offering

The tithe on crops in the Torah ended up being over 20 percent of a crop's yield, and it was essentially broken down into three components:

1. A portion of the firstfruits (*trumah gedolah*)
2. The first tithe (*ma'aser rishon*)
3. The second tithe (*ma'aser sheni*)

First, before anything else was done with the harvest, a portion of the firstfruits was separated from it. This is referred to in Hebrew as *trumah gedolah* (תרומה גדולה), which literally means "large heave offering." Deuteronomy 18:4 states, "The firstfruits of your grain, of your wine and of your oil, and the first fleece of your sheep, you shall give [the priest]." Although the Torah itself does not specify an actual amount that was to be given, the sages derived a rule of thumb from Ezekiel 45:13, which they understood as alluding to a minimum of one sixtieth of one's entire produce. Yet a farmer was free to give more than this amount as well:

> [This is] the amount of *trumah*: "The man with a good eye [i.e., the generous man] gives a fortieth"; Beit Shammai says, "One thirtieth." The average man one fiftieth and the man with a bad eye [i.e., the stingy man] gives one sixtieth. (m.*Trumot* 4:3)

The *trumah gedolah* from the firstfruits was taken first, before any other tithes were separated from the produce. In the times of the Temple, it was given to the priests.

First Tithe

After the *trumah gedolah* was set apart, the "first tithe" (*ma'aser rishon,* מעשר ראשון) was separated. This is equal to one tenth of what was left of the harvest after the *trumah gedolah*, the large heave offering, was given. This is based on Numbers 18:24:

> The tithe of the people of Israel, which they present as a contribution to the LORD, I have given to the Levites for an inheritance. Therefore I have said of them that they shall have no inheritance among the people of Israel.

Because the Levites were given no land inheritance in Israel and were therefore unable to grow their own produce, they were given this tithe, the *ma'aser rishon*, to survive on. A farmer growing wheat, for example, after separating the *trumah gedolah*, would measure off 10 percent of his remaining wheat harvest for the Levites.

A few verse later the Torah commands:

> Moreover, you shall speak and say to the Levites, "When you take from the people of Israel the tithe that I have given you from them for your inheritance, then you shall present a contribution from it to the LORD, a tithe of the tithe." (Numbers 18:26)

The Levites were to give a tenth of the *ma'aser rishon* to the priests. This is called the *trumat ha-ma'aser* (תרומת המעשר), the "offering tithe." The first tithe, then, consisted of 10 percent to be given to the Levites, and they in turn gave a tenth of that to the priests.

Second Tithe

Last, there is the "second tithe," the *ma'aser sheni* (מעשר שני). The Torah commands:

> You shall tithe all the yield of your seed that comes from the field year by year. And before the LORD your God, in the place that he will choose, to make his name dwell there, you shall eat the tithe of your grain, of your wine, and of your oil, and the firstborn of your herd and flock,

that you may learn to fear the LORD your God always. And if the way is too long for you, so that you are not able to carry the tithe, when the LORD your God blesses you, because the place is too far from you, which the LORD your God chooses, to set his name there, then you shall turn it into money and bind up the money in your hand and go to the place that the LORD your God chooses and spend the money for whatever you desire—oxen or sheep or wine or strong drink, whatever your appetite craves. And you shall eat there before the LORD your God and rejoice, you and your household. (Deuteronomy 14:22–26)

This is the *ma'aser sheni*, the second 10 percent of what remains of the harvest after the *trumah gedolah*, the heave offering, and the *ma'aser rishon*, the first tithe, were removed. It was separated and either consumed directly in Jerusalem at the pilgrimage festivals by the one offering it or sold and the money used to buy food and drink to consume in Jerusalem at the pilgrimage festivals. It was kind of like a savings plan for celebrating the festivals.

Poor Tithe

The second tithe was actually distributed in two ways, depending on the year in the Sabbatical Year cycle. The Torah tells us in Leviticus 25 that every seven years the land was to lie fallow and be given a rest, during which no planting or harvesting was to be done. In Deuteronomy 14 we read,

At the end of every three years you shall bring out all the tithe of your produce in the same year and lay it up within your towns. And the Levite, because he has no portion or inheritance with you, and the sojourner, the fatherless, and the widow, who are within your towns, shall come and eat and be filled, that the LORD your God may bless you in all the work of your hands that you do. (Deuteronomy 14:28–29)

During the third and sixth years of the seven-year cycle, this second tithe became the *ma'aser ani* (מעשר עני), the "poor tithe," which was distributed to those in need. Deuteronomy 26 even stipulates a declaration that was to go along with this offering.

Therefore, on the first, second, fourth, and fifth years, the second tithe was eaten in Jerusalem, but on the third and sixth years it was distributed to the needy, while in the seventh year no tithes were separated at all, because it was the Sabbatical Year.

Tithing without a Temple

In order to be carried out to the fullest of the Torah's injunctions, tithing was directly dependent on the Temple. Today, because there is no Temple, this presents a problem. The rabbis have ruled that while tithes are still required to be separated, they are to be handled a bit differently.[12]

The *trumah gedolah* is separated, but it is no longer given to the priests. Instead it is buried, as a precaution, so that no one will eat it by mistake. The *ma'aser rishon*, the first tithe, is also separated, and it can either be given to a Levite, as when the Temple was standing, or simply be kept by the owner. The *trumat ha-ma'aser* (the tithe from the first tithe) that the Levite normally gave to the priest is now buried, once again to ensure that no one will eat it.

As for the *ma'aser sheni*, the second tithe, in the first, second, fourth, and fifth years of the Sabbatical cycle, when it was normally eaten in Jerusalem, it is now redeemed with a coin and may then be distributed or sold as one wishes. In the third and sixth years of the Sabbatical cycle, the second tithe is still given to the poor, just as when the Temple was standing.

While some of these procedures might sound strange or even contradictory to the Torah, the rabbis have spent a great deal of time deliberating on these rulings in an effort to figure out how to properly deal with the tithing system in an era in which the Temple is no longer standing.

These three components—the large heave offering, the first tithe with its subsequent tithe given by the Levites, and the second tithe—form the major tithing system of the Torah, but there were more tithe-like commandments in the Torah than these. In the next chapter we will examine the many other tithe-like commandments on agricultural crops.

To review:

- Torah tithes were only applicable to crops.
- Torah tithes were only applicable to what was grown in the land of Israel.[13]
- Most authorities ruled that biblically Torah tithes were only applicable to grain (wheat, barley, oats, spelt, and rye), wine (grapes), and oil (olives).[14]
- It was rabbinically forbidden to consume un-tithed produce.

The three main components of the basic tithe system:

- The *trumah gedolah:* a portion of the firstfruits given to the priests
- The *ma'aser rishon* ("first tithe"): given to the Levites
- The *ma'aser sheni* ("second tithe"): consumed in Jerusalem or given to the poor, depending on the Sabbatical Year cycle

For a chart detailing all these tithes and how they are distributed based upon the Sabbatical Year cycle, see Appendix 1.

3
Other Tithe-like Commandments

Beyond the main tithing system of the Torah, there are numerous regulations that stipulate other tithe-like practices on agricultural business in the land of Israel.

Firstfruits

There is the mitzvah of giving the *bikkurim* (ביכורים), "firstfruits," to the priest. When the first of the crops began to sprout, the farmer went out into his field and tied a string around the firstlings and declared them *bikkurim*. Although the Torah does not stipulate an amount to be given, the sages set a minimum quantity of one sixtieth of the harvest, with no maximum.[15]

Unlike the *trumah gedolah* (the large heave offering), the *bikkurim* applied only to the seven species of Deuteronomy 8:8 (wheat, barley, grapes, figs, pomegranates, olives, and honey, which refers to dates), and unlike the *trumah gedolah*, which was simply given to a priest in any location, *bikkurim* were actually brought to the Temple and offered before the altar:

> When you come into the land that the LORD your God is giving you for an inheritance and have taken possession of it and live in it, you shall take some of the first of all the fruit of the ground, which you harvest from your land that the LORD your God is giving you, and you shall put it in a basket, and you shall go to the place that the LORD your God will choose, to make his name to dwell there. (Deuteronomy 26:1–2)

The Torah goes on to specify a detailed process for this offering complete with a liturgical declaration that was to be made at the Temple. The firstfruits were to be brought to the Temple anytime between the festival of Shavu'ot and Sukkot. They could even be brought as late as Hanukkah, but if they were brought after Sukkot, it was ruled that no declaration was to be recited.[16]

The journey to bring the firstfruits to the Temple was an event in and of itself. The people walked in a celebratory fashion with accompanying flute players, led by an ox whose horns were decorated with silver and gold complete with olive branches atop his head. The firstfruits themselves were placed in fancy baskets.[17]

Firstfruits were taken from the seven species of Deuteronomy 8:8 that had been grown in the land of Israel.[18] Without a Temple the practice of firstfruits is no longer observed.

Corners and Gleanings of the Field

There are also regulations about what was or was not to be picked up or gathered in a field:

> When you reap the harvest of your land, you shall not reap your field right up to its edge, neither shall you gather the gleanings after your harvest. (Leviticus 19:9)

This verse actually gives two separate commandments. First, the corners or edges of the field were not to be harvested but instead left for the poor. This is called *pe'ah* (פאה), which literally means "corner." Although the Torah does not specify an amount to be given, the sages said that a minimum of one sixtieth of the field was to be left as *pe'ah*.[19]

Second, the one who reaped his field was not permitted to go back and gather that which had fallen from his hand or sickle during the harvesting process. This is called *leket* (לקט), which literally translates as "gleanings."

Reading the next verse we find more mitzvot regarding a vineyard:

> You shall not strip your vineyard bare, neither shall you gather the fallen grapes of your vineyard. You shall leave

them for the poor and for the sojourner: I am the LORD your God. (Leviticus 19:10)

Traditionally, this has been interpreted as forbidding the gathering of *olelot* (עוללות), the smaller, immature clusters of grapes still on the vine, or *peret* (פרט), clusters of grapes that fell during the picking process.[20] These were all to be left for the poor and the stranger.

Additionally, the Torah gives injunctions regarding forgotten sheaves:

> When you reap your harvest in your field and forget a sheaf in the field, you shall not go back to get it. It shall be for the sojourner, the fatherless, and the widow, that the LORD your God may bless you in all the work of your hands. (Deuteronomy 24:19)

These forgotten sheaves are referred to in rabbinic literature as *shich'chah* (שכחה). They include both that which was picked and then left as well as that which was still attached because it had been overlooked by the harvesters.[21]

While all agree that the commandments of *pe'ah*, *leket*, *olelot*, *peret*, and *shich'chah* were, and are, applicable within the land of Israel, the sages debate how much these should be observed outside the land.[22] All these precepts are considered in force today and are still observed.

New Trees

> When you come into the land and plant any kind of tree for food, then you shall regard its fruit as forbidden. Three years it shall be forbidden to you; it must not be eaten. And in the fourth year all its fruit shall be holy, an offering of praise to the LORD. But in the fifth year you may eat of its fruit, to increase its yield for you: I am the LORD your God. (Leviticus 19:23–25)

Leviticus gives regulations concerning new fruit trees. This is called the law of *orlah* (ערלה). *Orlah* means "blocked" and refers to the forbidden fruit of the first three years of a tree's growth. The three years are calculated from *Tu Bishvat* (New Year of the

Trees), which is on the fifteenth of Shevat. Traditional halachic ruling states that the fruit was to be burned. This law is observed even today, both in and outside the land of Israel.

In the fourth year, the fruit was called *neta reva'i* (נטע רבעי) and was to be eaten in Jerusalem in a celebratory meal before HaShem. If this was not possible, the fruit was redeemed and the money then spent in Jerusalem on food in the same manner as with the *ma'aser sheni*, the second tithe. Today the law of *neta reva'i* is considered by most as applicable only within the land of Israel, and in practice the fruit is redeemed and may then be consumed.

The Sabbatical and Jubilee Years

> For six years you shall sow your land and gather in its yield, but the seventh year you shall let it rest and lie fallow, that the poor of your people may eat; and what they leave the beasts of the field may eat. You shall do likewise with your vineyard, and with your olive orchard. (Exodus 23:10–11)

In the seventh year, called the *shmittah* year, all agricultural work was to cease. *Shmittah* (שמיטה) is Hebrew for "release," because in this year all crops were released—that is, they became ownerless so that the poor could come and glean. In addition to a number of non-agricultural commandments, the Torah lists four prohibitions in Leviticus 25 related to agriculture in the seventh year: *zorea* ("sowing," זורע), *zomer* ("pruning," זומר), *kotzer* ("reaping," קוצר), and *botzer* ("picking," בוצר). The field owner was not permitted to cultivate the soil or sow seed, prune, reap, or gather the harvest. The fields, vineyards, and fruit trees became ownerless, and individuals could gather and harvest only what was needed for immediate use.

This practice was repeated in the *yovel* ("Jubilee," יובל) year—the fiftieth year after a cycle of seven *shmittah* years. This meant that for two years in a row (with a *shmittah* year in the forty-ninth year and a *yovel* in the fiftieth), the four prohibitions of the *shmittah* year applied. Additionally in the *yovel*, all property outside any walled city reverted back to its original owner; this included agricultural land. The Torah does not set up a capitalist economy but rather one that is solely focused on the love of God and the love of one's neighbor.

The Sabbatical Year and the Jubilee Year were observed only in the land of Israel.[23] Now that we live in a period without a Temple, while the Sabbatical Year is still observed, the Jubilee Year is not.

Challah

There are even tithe-like commandments that reach into the kitchen. Numbers 15 speaks of tithing the first of the dough:

> The LORD spoke to Moses, saying, "Speak to the people of Israel and say to them, When you come into the land to which I bring you and when you eat of the bread of the land, you shall present a contribution to the LORD. Of the first of your dough you shall present a loaf as a contribution; like a contribution from the threshing floor, so shall you present it. Some of the first of your dough you shall give to the LORD as a contribution throughout your generations." (Numbers 15:17–21)

A portion of the first of the dough made from each year's crops was to be baked into a loaf and given to the priests for consumption. Therefore, even the non-farmer offered up a sort of firstfruits. This mitzvah was considered so important that its performance is said by the Prophet Ezekiel in 44:30 to cause a blessing to rest on one's house. The portion of the dough for the priest was called *challah* ("portion," חלה), and the mitzvah is called "the separation of challah."

Torah Club: Depths of the Torah explains:

> The Torah requires a person making bread to set aside a *challah* of dough from each batch as a type of *trumah* for the priesthood. A *challah* of dough set aside for the priesthood has the same sanctity as the *trumah* of the threshing floor. This means that only the priesthood and their families could eat it and only in a state of ritual purity.

> The Torah does not prescribe a minimum size for the *challah* removed from the batch of bread. Like the corner

of the field, it leaves the measure unspecified. The rabbis, however, provided some measurements. According to Jewish law, a batch of dough must be at least an omer of flour (2.33 quarts or 2.2 liters) before it is subject to the law of *challah*. The size of the *challah* portion must be at least a twenty-fourth of the total batch. In modern observance, when the *challah* does not actually go to the priests, smaller token-sized portions are side aside.

The sages specified that the dough must be made from the flour of the five grains produced in the land of Israel: wheat, spelt, barley, rye, and oats. The Torah makes the commandment of setting aside *challah* specifically incumbent within the land: "When you eat of the food of the land." The commandment "to set aside the *challah* portion for the priests" applies to Jewish people in the land of Israel with the priesthood and Levitical system in place. Rabbinic law, however, broadened the command to apply to all lands in every time lest the principle be forgotten. Since the *challah* is a form of *trumah*, the law does not apply to God-fearing Gentiles. Gentiles are exempt from setting aside both agricultural tithes and *trumah*.

Religious Jews still set aside a *challah* portion from large batches of bread dough today. Instead of giving it to the priesthood, however, the baker burns the *challah* portion in the oven or in the fire. Because the *challah* portion has the status of priestly *trumah*, the priests cannot eat it unless they are in a state of ritual purity. Therefore, the *challah* set aside from each batch of bread dough has no practical purpose. Even if a person gave it to a priest, under current circumstances, the priest and his family are Levitically unclean and will remain so until the ceremony of purification with ashes of the red heifer is reinstituted. The law is further discussed in tractates *Challah* and *Orlah*.[24]

Challah bread now refers to the braided Sabbath bread, but it originally meant the *challah* portion which had been removed from the dough and burned. So beyond the main tithing system of the

Torah, we see these five offerings among the numerous tithe-like regulations regarding crops and agriculture. In the next chapter we are going to look at a few more tithe-like commandments that are related not to crops but to livestock. There is even one consisting of a half-shekel.

4
Non-Crop Tithes

In chapter 2 we saw that all the tithes in the Torah were specifically related to crops of the field. And indeed, this is true of the main tithing system of the Torah discussed in that chapter. There are, however, a few tithe-like commandments that apply to non-produce items.

Firstborn

Like the command to offer the firstfruits of the harvest, there is also the Torah requirement to offer up the firstborn (*bechor*, בכור) of animals. God told Aaron and the priests,

> Everything that opens the womb of all flesh, whether man or beast, which they offer to the LORD, shall be yours. Nevertheless, the firstborn of man you shall redeem, and the firstborn of unclean animals you shall redeem. And their redemption price (at a month old you shall redeem them) you shall fix at five shekels in silver, according to the shekel of the sanctuary, which is twenty gerahs. But the firstborn of a cow, or the firstborn of a sheep, or the firstborn of a goat, you shall not redeem; they are holy. You shall sprinkle their blood on the altar and shall burn their fat as a food offering, with a pleasing aroma to the LORD. But their flesh shall be yours, as the breast that is waved and as the right thigh are yours. (Numbers 18:15–18)

While the firstborn of man was to be redeemed, the firstborn of the livestock was not, with the one exception being the firstborn donkey, which was redeemed with a lamb. The firstborn animal was offered up on the altar in Jerusalem, and the priest was required to eat its flesh there. If the animal developed a blemish, however, it was not offered up on the altar but was given to the priest nonetheless.

Today, without a Temple, the firstborn of an animal is usually left to graze by itself until it develops a blemish, and it is then given to a priest.[25]

Offering of Wool

There is also the mitzvah in Deuteronomy 18:4 to give "the first fleece of your sheep" to the priest. The sages ruled that this should be one sixtieth of all the fleece gathered in quantity, and it is still observed today in the land of Israel, where a portion of wool is given to the priests.[26]

Priestly Portions

Additionally, from every single kosher animal that was slaughtered for food, the priests were to receive portions:

> This shall be the priests' due from the people, from those offering a sacrifice, whether an ox or a sheep: they shall give to the priest the shoulder and the two cheeks and the stomach. (Deuteronomy 18:3)

Halachically this refers to the upper part of the right foreleg, the jowls along with the tongue, and the fourth stomach, known as the maw. There were no issues of ritual purity attached to these parts, so the priest could eat them anywhere himself or sell them if he desired.

This requirement is widely interpreted today as applicable only within the land of Israel, and it is still observed.[27]

Animal Tithe

Lastly, the Torah mentions a tithe on animals (*ma'aser behemah*, מעשר בהמה):

> Every tithe of herds and flocks, every tenth animal of all that pass under the herdsman's staff, shall be holy to the LORD. One shall not differentiate between good or bad, neither shall he make a substitute for it; and if he does substitute for it, then both it and the substitute shall be holy; it shall not be redeemed. (Leviticus 27:32–33)

This tithe was usually done once a year by leading the animals through a narrow opening through which only one animal at a time could fit. The farmer would then count and mark every tenth animal—thus the selection process would be totally random, and the farmer would not be selecting the best to keep for himself. If the animals were unblemished, they were offered up as peace offerings on the altar in Jerusalem, and the owner would eat of its flesh there. If they were blemished, they were not offered up and could be eaten anywhere.

This commandment is applicable both in the land of Israel and outside. The tithe on animals is not observed today, since there is no Temple.[28]

Half-Shekel Tax

There is one last non-crop tithe-like commandment: the half-shekel tax:

> Each one who is numbered in the census shall give this: half a shekel according to the shekel of the sanctuary (the shekel is twenty gerahs), half a shekel as an offering to the LORD. Everyone who is numbered in the census, from twenty years old and upward, shall give the LORD's offering. The rich shall not give more, and the poor shall not give less, than the half shekel, when you give the LORD's offering to make atonement for your lives. (Exodus 30:13–15)

This constituted an annual tax of one half-shekel to be paid to the Tabernacle and later to the Temple to aid in its upkeep. It was not actually a tithe, per se, because it was a fixed amount, no matter one's income. The half-shekel tax was paid by all males aged twenty years and older. It was collected in the month of Adar from all settlements both in and outside Israel, wherever the Jewish people lived, and then brought to the Temple in Jerusalem.[29] The half-shekel tax is not collected today without the presence of a Temple.[30]

While the majority of tithing laws in Israel were on agricultural crops, there were these few tithe-like mitzvot that dealt with non-produce items. When we add up all the tithes and tithe-like commandments, it can be extremely overwhelming to realize how much a farmer gave away. But we must keep in mind that HaShem was trying to teach us an important lesson through all these mitzvot.

5
Spiritual Significance

The Torah's vast laws on tithing can seem complicated to the uninitiated and even make the head of the expert dizzy at times. When all is said and done, the average Israelite involved in agriculture and livestock is giving away a lot more than just 10 percent in tithes. No doubt many observant Jewish farmers, both in the days of the Temple and today, have felt overwhelmed with the amount of Torah legislation surrounding tithing and the prospect of giving away so much of their livelihood.

Korah's Complaint

Torah Club: Depths of the Torah, in the weekly Torah portion Parashat Korach (Numbers 16:1–18:32), brings up an amusing story from *Midrash Shocher Tov* on this very topic. In the story Korah attempts to incite the people against Moses and Aaron by stating that the Aaronic priesthood has their hands in everything via the tithing system. This comical anecdote has Korah telling the story of a poor widow:

> A widow, the mother of two young daughters, started to plow her solitary field whose yield was just sufficient to keep body and soul together. Moses told her that it was forbidden to plow with an ox and ass together (Deuteronomy 22:10). When she began to sow, Moses told her not to sow with diverse seeds (Leviticus 19:19). When the first fruits appeared, Moses demanded she give them to the priests (Deuteronomy 26:2), and when she began to harvest the field, Moses reminded her to leave the gleanings and the corners of the field for the poor (Leviticus

23:22). When she was about to thresh the grain, Moses demanded the separations for the priests and the Levites (Numbers 18:8, 21). Unable to maintain herself from the field under such conditions, she sold it and purchased ewes. Once again, she knew no peace. When the firstling of the sheep was born, Aaron demanded it for the priests (Numbers 18:15). When she began to shear the sheep, Aaron claimed the initials sheerings (Deuteronomy 18:4). The widow thereupon decided to slaughter the sheep. This time Aaron came for the priestly portions (Deuteronomy 18:3). The widow then vehemently cried out: "If you persist in your demands, I consecrate the flesh to the Lord." "If so," Aaron replied, "the whole [animal] belongs to me." (Numbers 18:14). Aaron then took away all the meat, leaving the widow and her two daughters entirely unprovided for. (*Midrash Shocher Tov* 1:15)

The story illustrates that following the Torah commandments on tithing would not always have been easy. Again, the Torah demands more than just 10 percent—in fact, all things considered, it requires more than 20 percent.

Yet not only does God promise throughout his Word that he will provide for those who are obedient to his commandments, but also through these tithe commandments he is attempting to teach an important lesson.

The Earth Is the LORD's

We live in a day and age in which there is no Temple. In addition, most of us do not live in the land of Israel and are not involved in agriculture. Many reading this book may not even be Jewish. This means that most of the Torah's mitzvot on tithing don't apply to us. Yet the Torah tithing system does teach us important lessons about our possessions.

Psalm 24:1 teaches us that "the earth is the LORD's and the fullness thereof." God created the world, and it belongs to him, but at the same time he created it for us to enjoy and to utilize. It is also God who gives and who takes. If our harvest is successful, it is thanks to him; if it is not, possibly he is trying to teach us something.

One of God's biggest concerns for the children of Israel when they were about to enter into the bounty of the promised land is that they would become successful and forget who it was who really owned the land and brought blessings. In Deuteronomy 8 we read of HaShem's stern warning against this danger:

> Take care … lest, when you have eaten and are full and have built good houses and live in them, and when your herds and flocks multiply and your silver and gold is multiplied and all that you have is multiplied, then your heart be lifted up, and you forget the LORD your God, who brought you out of the land of Egypt, out of the house of slavery. … Beware lest you say in your heart, "My power and the might of my hand have gotten me this wealth." You shall remember the LORD your God, for it is he who gives you power to get wealth. (Deuteronomy 8:11–18)

Rabbi Hirsch writes on the message of tithing, "Man has no greater enemy than success."[31] When we forget the one who has gotten us to where we are, we are in trouble. Success, though obviously not always bad, has a way of clouding our minds with visions of grandeur and pride. Rabbi Hirsch feels that the purpose of all these tithing commandments teaches us two important lessons: first, we must not forget that HaShem is the owner of everything, and second, because he has given us possessions to take care of, we must neither neglect nor misuse them.

We are to take care of the precious gifts God gives us. Every time we have to give some of our possessions back to him, it reminds us of this important principle.

Trust in HaShem

The Israelites were required to have immense trust in their Father in heaven to provide for their needs. This reminds us of the Master's words in Matthew 6 about not being anxious for our lives or worrying about what we will eat or drink. He tells us, "Seek first the kingdom of God and his righteousness, and all these things will be added to you" (Matthew 6:33). God desires our hearts, and through the tithing system we indeed learn what our true priorities should be.

Although the Torah's system of tithing can seem confusing and even cumbersome, it teaches us valuable lessons about trusting in HaShem and his provision. We must always remember that it is our Father in heaven who provides our sustenance and bounty. When we are blessed, it is not because of the work of our own hands but because of his great care for his children. By regulating tithes on crops and other items, God was instilling in the Israelites an attitude of thankfulness and gratitude.

Having reviewed these details on the laws of tithing in Torah and the spiritual significance they teach us, we are now ready to examine how tithing was carried out in the era of the New Testament.

6
The Expansion of Tithing

It is in the Gospels and the Epistles that we see the outworking of the commandments as they were given in the Torah. Therefore, it is imperative when considering our own personal practice that we see how Yeshua and the apostles carried out these commandments and what importance they placed on them.

Tithes on Everything

To begin, consider the famous story of the Pharisee and the tax collector. The tax collector was in the Temple praying and beating his breast as he begged for mercy from God. The Pharisee, on the other hand, looked at the tax collector with disdain and boasted of all his deeds before HaShem. He prayed,

> God, I thank you that I am not like other men, extortioners, unjust, adulterers, or even like this tax collector. I fast twice a week; I give tithes of all that I get. (Luke 18:11–12)

John Lightfoot points out that the Pharisee's declaration "I give tithes on all that I get" is very similar to the declaration prescribed by the Torah in Deuteronomy for a person offering up the second tithe in the third and sixth year.[32] Deuteronomy 26:13 prescribes the recitation, "I have removed the sacred portion out of my house, and moreover, I have given it to the Levite, the sojourner, the fatherless, and the widow."

Notice that the Pharisee speaks of tithing on "all that I get." Here we find evidence that already by the Second Temple period, some groups were giving tithes not just on agricultural produce but on all forms of income. This practice is also reflected in the early Jewish-Christian document the *Didache*.[33]

Whether tithing on everything was considered going above and beyond the letter of the law or as following the Torah is a matter of debate. We have already seen that the Torah does not explicitly command tithing on all our possessions, but we also learned that the principle of tithing 10 percent on everything was established in Genesis with Abraham and Jacob. An early midrash even finds support for tithing beyond agricultural produce through a creative exegesis of the text. *Midrash Sifrei* quotes Deuteronomy 14:22:

> "You shall definitely tithe all your agricultural produce which comes forth in the field every year." From this we could deduce that only agricultural produce must be tithed. How can we deduce that it applies to loan interest, trading, and all other profits? From the word "all"; for the verse could have stated "your agricultural produce". What is the significance of "all"? To include loan interest, trading, and all other profits."[34]

Therefore it is possible that the Pharisee considered the tithing of everything to be a fulfillment of the Torah's commands and not going above and beyond. In any case, the Master's criticism was not directed at the Pharisee's pious actions but rather at his haughty attitude. It's not the deeds that were a problem but the spirit that was behind them.

Dill, Mint, and Cumin

In Matthew 23 the Master himself addressed some of the tithing practices of the Pharisees.

> Woe to you, scribes and Pharisees, hypocrites! For you tithe mint and dill and cumin, and have neglected the weightier matters of the law: justice and mercy and faithfulness. These you ought to have done, without neglecting the others. (Matthew 23:23)

We find an echo of this teaching in Luke 11:42:

Woe to you Pharisees! For you tithe mint and rue and every herb, and neglect justice and the love of God. These you ought to have done, without neglecting the others.

In this passage Yeshua criticized the Pharisees for being so scrupulous about their tithing practices yet at the same time neglecting the weightier matters of the law. As was mentioned earlier, most authorities ruled that the laws for tithing crops only applied to grain, wine, and oil. Garden herbs such as dill, mint, and cumin would have been outside this requirement, and therefore tithing on them would have been considered above and beyond the letter of the commandment. They were required to be tithed only per rabbinic enactment.[35]

Yet we see once again that Yeshua did not dismiss this scrupulous practice outright—in fact, he almost commended it. He concluded by saying, "These you ought to have done, without neglecting the others." His issue was that for this group of Pharisees, tithing mint, dill, and cumin was done at the expense of the much weightier principles of Torah, which involved loving one's neighbor.

We see that by the Second Temple period, the sages of Israel had begun to expand the tithing mitzvot beyond their application in the letter of the law. Not only was tithing extended to one's income, but even the tithing for produce was expanded beyond grain, wine, and oil. In both of these stories from the Gospels, the Master did not come against the expansion of the tithing mitzvot but rather wanted to ensure that they were done with the proper spirit and balance.

In the next chapter we'll take a further look at Yeshua's words on tithing.

7

Tithing Commandments in the Gospels

T hroughout the Gospels we find allusions to tithing mitzvot. Sometimes these mitzvot are explicitly mentioned and other times implicitly. These references have important implications as we consider our tithing practice.

Feeding of the Four Thousand and Five Thousand

One of the major issues that arose in the days of the apostles concerning the tithing commandments was knowing what to do if one was unsure whether or not the food he or she was eating had been tithed. Remember that according to rabbinic exegesis of the Torah, not only was tithing required, but it was also forbidden to eat food from which the tithe had not been taken.

When food such as bread was thought to have been produced from grains that had not been tithed, it was referred to as *demai* (דמאי) and was considered consecrated and forbidden to be used as ordinary food. While almost every farmer removed the *trumah gedolah* (the large heave offering), some, in an effort to get more profit from their harvest, did not remove the first or second tithe. Having studied the vast amount of agricultural regulations on the Israelite farmer, we can understand why some might have resorted to this practice. So in the case of *demai* (doubtfully tithed produce), very pious Jews would remove one hundredth of the food, as a precaution, and discard it so that no one could eat it.

New Testament and rabbinic scholar David Instone-Brewer has proposed that this is the situation going on in the stories of the feeding of the four and five thousand in the Gospels.[36] At the end of Matthew's account of the feeding of the five thousand, we read,

> They all ate and were satisfied. And they took up twelve baskets full of the broken pieces left over. (Matthew 14:20)

Almost identical language is found in Matthew 15:37 in the account of the feeding of the four thousand:

> They all ate and were satisfied. And they took up seven baskets full of the broken pieces left over.

These same details are given in the parallel accounts of Mark, Luke, and John. Instone-Brewer believes that the reason there were leftovers is that the people considered the food *demai* (doubtfully tithed) and thus separated a portion to either be given to a priest or destroyed so that no one would eat it. Therefore, this seems to be an example of the disciples of Yeshua being scrupulous about the mitzvah of tithing.

Should Priests Tithe?

Another issue of controversy in the Second Temple period surrounding the tithing system was whether or not priests were required to tithe on their own crops and produce. Some scholars have suggested that this tithing debate is the contextual background of the parable of the vineyard in Luke 20.[37] To find out why, let's first read the parable:

> He began to tell the people this parable: "A man planted a vineyard and let it out to tenants and went into another country for a long while. When the time came, he sent a servant to the tenants, so that they would give him some of the fruit of the vineyard. But the tenants beat him and sent him away empty-handed. And he sent another servant. But they also beat and treated him shamefully, and sent him away empty-handed. And he sent yet a third. This one also they wounded and cast out. Then the

owner of the vineyard said, 'What shall I do? I will send my beloved son; perhaps they will respect him.' But when the tenants saw him, they said to themselves, 'This is the heir. Let us kill him, so that the inheritance may be ours.' And they threw him out of the vineyard and killed him. What then will the owner of the vineyard do to them? He will come and destroy those tenants and give the vineyard to others." When they heard this, they said, "Surely not!" But he looked directly at them and said, "What then is this that is written: 'The stone that the builders rejected has become the cornerstone'? Everyone who falls on that stone will be broken to pieces, and when it falls on anyone, it will crush him." The scribes and the chief priests sought to lay hands on him at that very hour, for they perceived that he had told this parable against them, but they feared the people. (Luke 20:9–19)

Notice that at the end of the parable, it was the Temple authorities, that is, the scribes and priests, who were offended at the Master's parable. They had figured out that he was talking about them.

The parable illustrates a situation in which the tenants of the vineyard—in this case the priests—were not giving back a portion of the fruit to the landowner. The language in the story is reminiscent of the idea of tithing, in which the farmer gives back to God a portion from the land that in reality belongs to HaShem himself.

In Numbers we read that the tithes of the Israelites were the inheritance of the priests and the Levites and that in turn the priests and Levites would not be given a land inheritance within Israel:

> The tithe of the people of Israel, which they present as a contribution to the LORD, I have given to the Levites for an inheritance. Therefore I have said of them that they shall have no inheritance among the people of Israel. (Numbers 18:24)

Although the Torah set up this situation for the sons of Levi, by the end of the Second Temple period, the priestly class had become very wealthy and as a result many among them were large land owners. Therefore, the question arose as to whether or not tithes should be paid on crops grown on their own land. An ancient midrash on Deuteronomy called *Sifrei* speaks to this situation:

> The Sages said: The [produce] stores for the children of Hanan [the high priest Annas, Luke 3:2; John 18:13] were destroyed three years before the rest of the Land of Israel because they failed to set aside tithes from their produce, for they interpreted [Deuteronomy 14:22] *Thou shalt surely tithe … and thou shalt eat* as excluding the seller, and *The increase of the seed* as excluding the buyer. (*Sifrei* 105)[38]

The above translation comes from Reuven Hammer. He additionally includes a note on the text stating,

> These were stores set up by a wealthy priest to sell items used in sacrifices. They followed their own interpretation and left tithing to the farmers who raised the produce.[39]

Randall Buth and Brian Kvasnica comment on the text, saying,

> With a smooth exegesis of Deuteronomy 14:22, the priests were able to gain both from having land tithe-free as well as giving their customers, the buyers, the ease of not worrying about whether or not the produce had been tithed on.[40]

With this interpretation, the priests could be totally free from the obligation to tithe. Yet tithe evasion was just the tip of the iceberg when it came to the injustices and corruptions of the priesthood in the days of Yeshua. We have ample literary evidence from the period that points to the ungodly character of the priesthood.

It is not only tithe evasion that Yeshua was attacking here but flagrant disregard for God's Torah and the overarching principles of the commandments. This parable demonstrates that Yeshua took the commandment of tithing very seriously and that disregard of the tithing laws could provide a window into the corrupt character of an individual.

Half-Shekel Tax

Although the half-shekel tax is not a tithe but more of a tax (as we pointed out in chapter 4), let's examine a passage in the Gospels in which this commandment comes up:

> When they came to Capernaum, the collectors of the two-drachma [half-shekel] tax went up to Peter and said, "Does your teacher not pay the tax?" He said, "Yes." And when he came into the house, Yeshua spoke to him first, saying, "What do you think, Simon? From whom do kings of the earth take toll or tax? From their sons or from others?" And when he said, "From others," Yeshua said to him, "Then the sons are free. However, not to give offense to them, go to the sea and cast a hook and take the first fish that comes up, and when you open its mouth you will find a shekel. Take that and give it to them for me and for yourself." (Matthew 17:24–27)

Regardless of whether or not Yeshua felt that he was exempt from the tax because of his special status as God's Son, he paid it, albeit not without some humorous dramatics. Peter, the burly fisherman accustomed to big nets and boats, probably did not appreciate being asked to go fishing with a pole.

Additionally, New Testament scholar Mark Nanos suggests that the half-shekel tax is the same tax that Paul asked Gentiles to pay in Romans 13:6–7.[41] Once again we see the obedience of the apostolic community toward the tithing and tithe-like commandments of the Torah.

These examples from the Gospels point to the fact that Yeshua and his disciples were indeed concerned with the commandments surrounding tithing. To them it would be unthinkable to thrust aside tithing mitzvot. But did they go so far as to say that through tithing and charity one would be blessed with an abundance of wealth?

8
Measure for Measure

Before we leave the Gospels and examine tithing in the rest of the New Testament, it is important that we challenge the principle of tithing and the prosperity doctrine. This concept is usually based on Yeshua's words regarding "measure for measure." Let's examine the passages containing these teachings in their original context from a Messianic Jewish perspective.

Measure for Measure

> Judge not, and you will not be judged; condemn not, and you will not be condemned; forgive, and you will be forgiven; give, and it will be given to you. Good measure, pressed down, shaken together, running over, will be put into your lap. For with the measure you use it will be measured back to you. (Luke 6:37–38)

Prosperity teachers cite this verse as proof that Yeshua was saying that the more we give (specifically in tithing), the more we get back, but in reality the context offers no proof whatsoever for this doctrine. Rather, Yeshua was teaching a common rabbinic principle of his day called "measure for measure." This is clarified even more fully in Matthew's version:

> With the judgment you pronounce you will be judged, and with the measure you use it will be measured to you. (Matthew 7:2)

In reality these passages teach that if we judge others, we will be judged by God. If we judge not, we will not be judged. If we forgive,

HaShem will be faithful to forgive us as well. The same concept appears at the end of the Lord's Prayer:

> If you forgive others their trespasses, your heavenly Father will also forgive you, but if you do not forgive others their trespasses, neither will your Father forgive your trespasses. (Matthew 6:14–15)

The line "give, and it will be given to you" in Luke's version refers to the aspects of judgment and forgiveness, not financial prosperity. When we express mercy to others, it will be expressed back to us in a full measure from God, beyond what we deserve. The measurements have nothing to do with money or finances but rather with character traits.

Jewish Background

This same principle is found in rabbinic literature. For example, in the Mishnah we read,

> In the measure with which a man measures it is meted out to him. (m.*Sotah* 1:7)

There is also a popular story about Hillel that expresses the same sentiment:

> He [Hillel] moreover once saw a skull floating upon the face of the water. "Because," he said to it, "Thou didst drown others, they have drowned thee, and they that drowned thee shall be drowned too." (b.*Sukkah* 53a)

The principle of "measure for measure" is found throughout the Tanach: Just as Miriam waited for her brother Moses to see what would become of him after he was placed in the basket, so Israel waited for Miriam to be cleansed from leprosy before continuing their journey in the wilderness.[42] Just as Moses, at the time of the exodus, personally concerned himself with fulfilling Israel's promise to Joseph to bring his bones back to the land of Israel for burial, so it was that HaShem honored Moses by burying him himself.[43] And just as the Egyptians sought to drown Israel's baby boys in the Nile, so they were drowned in the Red Sea.[44]

In the Luke passage the Master alludes to a passage in Malachi:

> Bring the full tithes into the storehouse, that there may be food in my house. And thereby put me to the test, says the LORD of hosts, if I will not open the windows of heaven for you and pour down for you a blessing until there is no more need. (Malachi 3:10)

While at first glance this seems to perpetuate the idea that Yeshua was here referring to tithing, let's remember a few things. First, the obvious context of the Master's message is the perpetuation of kindness. Yeshua used the principle of the Malachi passage: when we do good, God will return good to us in an overabounding manner. Second, although Malachi clearly establishes that when the Jewish people do tithe, God will bless them, we must remember that he is speaking of the Torah system of tithing, which was on agriculture and not on income.

Torah Club: Voice of the Prophets explains:

> [Yeshua is teaching us] to pardon others, to be merciful, withhold judgment and condemnation, and to give generously to those in need. He said, "Give, and it will be given to you. They will pour into your lap a good measure—pressed down, shaken together, and running over. For by your standard of measure it will be measured to you in return" (Luke 6:38). The Apostle Paul echoes the same sentiment when he says, "He who sows sparingly will also reap sparingly, and he who sows bountifully will also reap bountifully" (2 Corinthians 9:6). Nevertheless, we should beware religious fundraisers that encourage us to test God by supporting their causes or ministries with generous donations. The principles of the kingdom of heaven cannot be reduced to marketing schemes.[45]

Yeshua's words about "measure for measure" are not about becoming rich through generosity or gaining immense prosperity through tithing. To use these passages to promote a prosperity doctrine is to take them completely out of their context. Instead, the Master's words demonstrate that God often behaves toward us in the same manner that we behave toward our fellow man. It is about the multiplication of kindness, not of financial blessing.

Now that we have a firm understanding of the fact that Yeshua and his disciples upheld the tithing mitzvot, we might ask some questions: What about Paul and the rest of the writers of the New Testament? Did they also observe the laws of tithing? What importance did they place on these mitzvot?

9
Allusions to Tithing in the Epistles

There are a number of allusions to tithing commandments in the Epistles. While these references are used more symbolically than literally, they do point to the practice of tithing among the early believers.

Challah

In his letter to the Romans, Paul mentions the commandment of *challah* from Numbers 15. This is the commandment that states that a portion of the first of each year's dough was to be given to the priest. This then made the rest of the dough for that year acceptable to use. Incidentally, this is one of the few tithing commandments that even individuals in the Diaspora participated in during the Second Temple period.[46] Therefore, as a Diaspora Jew himself, the Apostle Paul would have been familiar with this practice and would personally have fulfilled this mitzvah himself.

In Romans 11:16 he writes,

> If the dough offered as firstfruits is holy, so is the whole lump, and if the root is holy, so are the branches.

The firstfruits of the dough represent Israel. If Israel is indeed holy, then so is the rest of the dough—the greater commonwealth of Israel, made up of the Gentiles throughout the world who have joined themselves to Israel through Messiah. Here Paul seems to be drawing in ideas from Leviticus 6:18 as well, where it is stated concerning the holy offerings, "Whatever touches them shall become holy." The whole passage is comprised of a rabbinic style of exegesis in which different texts of the Tanach are strung together to form a singular idea.

Firstfruits

There are a number of texts that speak to the commandment of the firstfruits (*bikkurim*). The imagery in Romans 8 appears to refer to the first outpouring of the Spirit:

> Not only the creation, but we ourselves, who have the firstfruits of the Spirit, groan inwardly as we wait eagerly for adoption as sons, the redemption of our bodies. (Romans 8:23)

Later, in Romans 16:5, Epaenetus is referred to as "the first convert to Messiah in Asia." In other words, he is the firstfruits of believers from among the Gentiles in Asia. In 1 Corinthians 16:15 Stephanas' household is described as the firstfruits of converts of Achaia. Similar imagery of firstfruits is brought forth in James and in the book of Revelation picturing all believers (both Jew and Gentile) in Messiah:

> Of his own will he brought us forth by the word of truth, that we should be a kind of firstfruits of his creatures. (James 1:18)

> It is these who have not defiled themselves with women, for they are virgins. It is these who follow the Lamb wherever he goes. These have been redeemed from mankind as firstfruits for God and the Lamb. (Revelation 14:4)

The picture of firstfruits seems a fitting one to describe Jewish and Gentile believers in Messiah, because just as the actual firstfruits of the crops began to be brought to the Temple at the feast of Shavu'ot, so did the early believing community begin bringing in large numbers at the outpouring of the Holy Spirit in Acts 2 during the festival of Shavu'ot and beyond. Therefore, the firstfruits create the perfect analogy to describe the incoming members of the Apostolic Messianic community.

Paul also brings up the imagery of firstfruits to describe the resurrection:

> Messiah has been raised from the dead, the firstfruits of those who have fallen asleep. For as by a man came death, by a man has come also the resurrection of the dead. For as in Adam all die, so also in Messiah shall all be made alive. But each in his own order: Messiah the firstfruits, then at his coming those who belong to Messiah. (1 Corinthians 15:20–23)

The firstfruits provide a very appropriate metaphor here as well, because just as the farmer must have faith when he ties off and dedicates a portion of the first of his crops that HaShem will provide a full harvest for him, in the same way we must have faith in the final resurrection of the dead because of the firstfruits that we have in Messiah Yeshua. Firstfruits are not only a symbol of tithing and giving thanks but also of hope and promise.

By Paul and the writer of Revelation employing this imagery so frequently, we can no doubt assume that this commandment was important to them and impressed not only upon their minds but in their practice as well.

Abraham and Levi

For one last example of the tithe commandment in the New Testament, we turn to the book of Hebrews:

> Those descendants of Levi who receive the priestly office have a commandment in the law to take tithes from the people, that is, from their brothers, though these also are descended from Abraham. But this man [that is, Melchizedek] who does not have his descent from them received tithes from Abraham and blessed him who had the promises. It is beyond dispute that the inferior is blessed by the superior. In the one case tithes are received by mortal men, but in the other case, by one of whom it is testified that he lives. One might even say that Levi himself, who receives tithes, paid tithes through Abra-

ham, for he was still in the loins of his ancestor when Melchizedek met him. (Hebrews 7:5–10)

The basic gist of this passage is that the priesthood of Melchizedek is greater than the priesthood of Aaron. This is evidenced by the fact that although Aaron was a descendant of Abraham, Abraham himself tithed to Melchizedek. What we should be careful not to infer here is that because the Melchizedek priesthood is greater, the Aaronic priesthood is no longer important.

First, we should note that the priesthood of Melchizedek cannot replace the Aaronic priesthood. The priesthood of Melchizedek existed first, and therefore it would be illogical to propose that it suddenly replaced something that was created after it. Second, what Hebrews is trying to do is show an order of sanctification and holiness. Just because the Aaronic priesthood is lower on the scale does not prove that it is obsolete. In the same way, the honor we show to our parents is greater than the honor we would show to a sibling. Yet this does not mean that we don't need to honor the sibling at all—just that he is on a different level.

While these verses do show the superiority of the Melchizedek priesthood, it does not in any way abolish the Aaronic priesthood and therefore does not abolish the tithing commandments that are so heavily dependent upon it. Those commandments are indeed perpetual throughout all generations.

Throughout the New Testament Epistles, we see allusions to the tithing commandments of the Torah. Although these are not referring to the commandments in a literal way but rather using them to illustrate concepts in the gospel, they still indicate that the apostles observed the tithing commandments and held them in high regard. This, in turn, was the attitude and spirit of the entire early believing community as is evidenced by early Jewish-Christian non-canonical literature.

10
Tithing in Early Jewish-Christian Literature

In order to get an idea of how much importance the early believers placed on the tithing commandments of Torah, it is important to examine some of the early Jewish-Christian non-canonical literature that was written around the same time as the New Testament. We will examine both the *Didache* and *1 Clement*.

Didache

The *Didache*, whose name means "teaching," is considered by scholars to be the earliest written work by believers apart from the New Testament. It was written perhaps as early as the middle of the first century. There is even a church tradition that it goes back to the twelve disciples themselves, with its full title being *The Teaching of the Lord through the Twelve Apostles to the Gentiles*. It is a collection of instructions intended for new Gentile believers in Messiah.

In it we get a glimpse of what tithing halachah may have looked like for Gentiles in the earliest believing communities. Remember that most of the Torah's tithing and tithe-like commandments are, for the most part, not incumbent upon non-Jews, so it appears that the *Didache* attempts to reinterpret some of these commandments for Gentiles. In a section dedicated to tithing instructions, we read,

> Every true prophet who wants to live among you is entitled to his sustenance. Likewise, a true teacher is also entitled, just as the worker is entitled to his sustenance. Therefore, you shall take every first part of the produce

of the wine press and threshing floor, and of both cattle and sheep, and give it to the prophets, because they are your high priests. But if you do not have a prophet, give it to the poor. When you make a batch of bread dough, take the first part and give it according to the commandment. Likewise, when you open a vessel of wine or oil, take the first part and give it to the prophets. Also of money and clothing and any other possession, take the first part as it seems fitting to you, and give it according to the commandment. (*Didache* 13)

The form is much like what we read in rabbinic halachah of the period. Some scholars speculate that this section of the *Didache* was part of a Jewish oral tradition that circulated around the time of the destruction of the Temple and that it was subsequently placed in the *Didache* and reworked for its intended audience. It is difficult to know whether "firstfruits" here actually refers to firstfruits specifically or is an idiom for tithing in general.

Unlike the Torah in which the firstfruits were given to the priests, in the *Didache* the firstfruits were to be given to the prophets. As a parallel in Judaism, Huub van de Sandt and David Flusser point out that even after the destruction of the Temple, the rabbis encouraged the people to continue to tithe, and they speculate that tithes were then specifically given to Levites who were rabbis (that is, teachers) as well.[47]

The phrase "according to the commandment" appears twice: once in reference to the bread firstfruits, which appears to be alluding to the mitzvah of *challah*, and once in reference to the taking of firstfruits of all one's possessions, which could refer to the rabbinic interpretation of Deuteronomy 14:22 found in *Sifrei* that one is to tithe on everything.

As we pointed out, this seems to represent the halachic practice of Gentiles living outside Israel after the destruction of the Temple. According to both Acts 15 and rabbinic literature, most of the laws of tithing were not fully incumbent upon Gentile believers. Therefore, the *Didache*'s instructions were for Gentile believers, teaching them how they could participate in the commandments and principles of the Torah tithing system.

Torah Club: Unrolling the Scroll explains:

> The early believers were Torah keepers, and they wanted to continue keeping the commandment of *challah* even outside the land of Israel and even in the absence of descendants of Aaron. The *Didache* reports that the early believers used to separate the *challah* portion of their dough and give it to the prophets. The prophets among the early believers were itinerant teachers who traveled from one believing community to another, spreading the gospel and speaking under the inspiration of the Holy Spirit. They were not allowed to ask for money, and they depended on the generosity of the community to sustain their ministries.[48]

In the event that there were no prophets or ministers of the Word in a community, the *Didache* instructed its readers to give the first portions to the poor.

These instructions show that the earliest community of believers saw the importance of the tithing system and sought to perpetuate its observance even after the destruction of the Temple and with the influx of new Gentile believers. Although these ideas are picked up again in later documents of church history, the *Didache* seems to be the most grounded and rooted within Judaism itself and thus has in its words a ring of authenticity when it comes to the practice of the early believers.

Clement

Let's examine another passage from another early non-canonical apostolic text called the *First Epistle of Clement*. Clement was an early believer, perhaps one of the original disciples of Peter.

In his writings Clement, as did New Testament writers, used the tithe-like metaphor of firstfruits in an allegorical sense, but Clement used it to describe the Jewish people. When writing to the Corinthians, Clement quoted a passage from Deuteronomy to demonstrate how God had divided the nations of humanity but had chosen Israel as his own portion. He went on to quote an unknown source that speaks of God taking Israel out of the nations like a farmer taking the firstfruits from his threshing floor. Just as the firstfruits are set aside from the rest of the crop to be a holy gift to the LORD, so too Israel is set apart from the other nations to be God's holy people. He writes,

> "When the Most High divided the nations … His people Jacob became the portion of the LORD, and Israel the lot of His inheritance" (Deuteronomy 32:8–9). And in another place [it is said], "Behold, the LORD takes for Himself a nation out of the midst of the nations, just as a man takes the first fruits of his threshing floor, and from that nation shall come forth the most holy." (*1 Clement* 29:1–3)

We do not know where Clement found the verse about God taking Israel like "a man takes the first fruits," but it is a beautiful image. From the midst of Israel comes "the most holy," which might be a prophecy regarding the Messiah. Clement used the verse about Israel's elect status to encourage the Gentile believers in Corinth. "God has made us partakers in the blessings of His elect" (*1 Clement* 29:1), he tells them, and he says, "Seeing, therefore, that we are the portion of the Holy One, let us do all those things which pertain to holiness" (*1 Clement* 30:1). Although, once again, tithing is used in a metaphorical sense, it does show that Clement is quite familiar with the Torah's commandment of firstfruits.

It is evident from both the *Didache* and from *1 Clement* that the early believers continued to practice the mitzvot of tithing.

Tithing Among the Earliest Followers of Yeshua

We have seen throughout the Gospels and the Epistles and all the way to the book of Revelation, as well as in the *Didache* and *1 Clement*, that the theme of tithing appears quite frequently. It is spoken of both in a practical sense, such as in the Master's mention of it in Matthew 23, but more often in a metaphorical sense, as we see through Paul's letters. This constant mention of tithes and firstfruits proves that both Yeshua and his disciples as well as the entire early believing community considered tithing to be a matter of great importance.

Additionally, just because something is spoken of often in a metaphorical sense does not negate the original literal application. Judaism has for centuries allegorized the commandments and their meanings while at the same time insisting on staunch observance of the actual physical commandment. That's because for Judaism and the apostles, all these allusions and instructions are based on the tithing system as it is found in the Torah.

Tithing in the Torah was considered a way to honor God for his goodness and at the same time keep one's heart in a state of humility and submission. Both of these are frequent themes in the New Testament.

All this should weigh deeply on us as disciples of Messiah Yeshua as we seek out a tithing practice. Because the Master's and the apostles' practices were in line with Torah and the traditions of Judaism, we should consider these things heavily. Additionally, we should be sensitive to the distinctions between Jews and Gentiles in tithing responsibilities, as we see done in the *Didache*.

11
The Dangers of Materialism

We are going to take a brief detour from the topic of tithing and focus for a few chapters on the overarching biblical principle of charity. The Bible teaches that every person of faith should have a spirit of generosity, and nothing gets in the way of this more than the spirit of materialism. A look at this issue will lay some important groundwork for later chapters, in which we will talk about practical application.

In today's world we are inundated daily with the spirit of consumerism. From billboards to magazine ads to TV commercials, we receive a constant flood of voices that tell us, "You need this, and you need it now!" This very quickly leads us down the road to materialism and greed. We begin to lust for perishable things, and eventually we give less and less away for the sake of the kingdom of heaven. How often do we let temporary things, things which have no long-term or sometimes even short-term value, control our lives? Most of us struggle deeply with the idolatry of mammon.

The Idolatry of Mammon

> You shall have no other gods before me. … You shall not bow down to them or serve them, for I the LORD your God am a jealous God. (Exodus 20:3–5)

The children of Israel were to place nothing before the One who is not only the greatest of all but the source of everything that has ever existed. The Master picked up on this idea in his words about mammon. In Luke 16:13 he states,

No servant can serve two masters, for either he will hate the one and love the other, or he will be devoted to the one and despise the other. You cannot serve God and money.

"Money" here is the Hebrew word *mamon* (ממון), which has been preserved transliterated in the Greek text. It is most commonly used to refer to material possessions. Yeshua echoes the Torah in his warning to us not to have any other masters before HaShem.

Scholars have speculated as to the background of this passage in Luke; some have suggested that it reflects the language we find in rabbinic literature that talks about the halachic implications of being a "half slave."[49] The real-life half slave would be either half free and half a slave, or he would actually be the slave of two different masters. To say the least, such a situation would pose many difficult problems; a half slave really couldn't serve two masters fully.

Another parallel background to this saying of Yeshua's can be found in *Midrash Ruth*:

> Rabbi Shimon said: "… 'And the slave is free from his master' (Job 3:19). Man, while he lives, is the slave of two Masters: the slave of his Creator and the slave of his inclination. When he does the will of his Creator, he angers his inclination, and when he does the will of his inclination, he angers his Creator. When he dies, he is freed, a slave from his Master." (*Midrash Ruth* 3:14)

The background of this midrash is the unusual spelling of the word "formed" in Genesis 2:7: "The LORD God formed [*vayitzer*, וייצר] the man." This is the only place in the entire Torah in which the Hebrew word for "formed" (*vayitzer*) is spelled with a double *yod* (י). The sages thought that God was trying to teach something special here, so they decided that each *yod* stood for something that every man was subjected to. The first *yod* was for *yetzer* ("inclination," יצר), which denotes our desires, and the second stood for y*otzer* (יוצר), which means "Creator," that is, God himself. Everyone struggles their entire life between two priorities—God's and their own.

The Master tells us that we cannot serve material things, which include our own carnal desires, and at the same time serve HaShem. Rather, we must strive to serve only HaShem.

The Love of Money

> The love of money is a root of all kinds of evils. It is through this craving that some have wandered away from the faith and pierced themselves with many pangs. (1 Timothy 6:10)

It is often taught that money is the root of all evil, but a careful reading of the passage reveals that it is the *love* of money that is the problem and not wealth in itself. Oftentimes we long to obtain things that we can never possess. As C.S. Lewis states: "Of unattainable longings sour is the fruit."[50] This longing desire can cause us to do unthinkable things. But what if we possessed such a fervency for the things of God?

Lack of giving has become a real problem in the body of Messiah today. Craig Blomberg, who has devoted an entire book called *Neither Poverty nor Riches* to correcting the materialism in the church, writes:

> It is arguable that materialism is the single biggest competitor with authentic Christianity for the hearts and souls of millions in our world today, including many in the visible church.[51]

His book is loaded with shocking statistics as to the depravity that we in the West have fallen to in the area of giving. And those who call themselves disciples of Yeshua are among those at fault. For example, while the average American gives between 1.6 and 2.4 percent of his annual income to charity, believers do not fare much better at 2.4 percent. It has been estimated that if all those who called themselves followers of Messiah would simply give 10 percent of their income, world hunger could be cured.

Blomberg brings out the fact that for many years we in the West adhered to the Wesleyan principle of "Gain all you can, save all you can, give all you can." Yet sadly, after World War II things changed dramatically. Blomberg writes,

> Following the Second World War, however, North American and Western European countries (those with the greatest modern legacy of Christian values) experienced

unprecedented rates of economic growth and affluence. The decades of the 1950s and the 1960s would sow the seeds of a considerable shift in thinking and practice with respect to material possessions. Whereas many who lived through the Great Depression and two world wars were sympathetic to Wesley's approach, patterns of both saving and giving began to erode.[52]

We love our money, and we enjoy spending it on temporary things. Yet this does not pass over the watchful eye of our Father who is in heaven. The Master warns his followers in Luke 16:15:

> You are those who justify yourselves before men, but God knows your hearts. For what is exalted among men is an abomination in the sight of God.

Blessed to Be a Blessing

Yet to say that God does not bless his people materially for their good is wrong as well. From the very beginning of Israel's calling as a nation, God promised that he would bless them both spiritually and physically. However, we learn that this blessing was given so that they could in turn be a blessing to others:

> I will make of you a great nation, and I will bless you and make your name great, so that you will be a blessing. I will bless those who bless you, and him who dishonors you I will curse, and in you all the families of the earth shall be blessed. (Genesis 12:2–3)

Blessed to be a blessing to others. In fact, God blessed each one of the patriarchs with a substantial amount of wealth:

> The LORD has greatly blessed my master [Abraham], and he has become great. He has given him flocks and herds, silver and gold, male servants and female servants, camels and donkeys. (Genesis 24:35)

> Isaac sowed in that land and reaped in the same year a hundredfold. The LORD blessed him, and the man

became rich, and gained more and more until he became very wealthy. (Genesis 26:12–13)

[Jacob] increased greatly and had large flocks, female servants and male servants, and camels and donkeys. (Genesis 30:43)

HaShem desired to bless Israel, and he even did so as they left Egypt by causing the Egyptians to be favorable toward them so that they gave Israel their silver and gold:

The people of Israel had also done as Moses told them, for they had asked the Egyptians for silver and gold jewelry and for clothing. And the LORD had given the people favor in the sight of the Egyptians, so that they let them have what they asked. Thus they plundered the Egyptians. (Exodus 12:35–36)

But nowhere do we see an example of wealth becoming evil more quickly than in the affair of the golden calf. The very finery that HaShem had blessed Israel with from Egypt was now used to create an idolatrous calf.

The dangers of materialism are all around us, and the Master urges us to be on guard lest we end up trying to serve two masters. It is not money that is evil. After all, many individuals throughout the Bible were blessed with abundance from God himself. Rather, it is the love of money and the misuse of our possessions and wealth that gets us into trouble. This is why the Torah contains so many lessons and instructions guarding against a spirit of materialism.

12
Lessons from the Torah

Because of the dangers of materialism, HaShem has given his people instructions within his Torah to help us guard against the love of money. These principles and commandments help us keep our priorities straight and our eyes focused on our Father in heaven.

Manna—Daily Bread

One of the vehicles that HaShem used to teach the children of Israel about the dangers of hoarding and materialism is the manna in the wilderness:

> "Gather of it, each one of you, as much as he can eat. You shall each take an omer, according to the number of the persons that each of you has in his tent." And the people of Israel did so. They gathered, some more, some less. But when they measured it with an omer, whoever gathered much had nothing left over, and whoever gathered little had no lack. … And Moses said to them, "Let no one leave any of it over till the morning." But they did not listen to Moses. Some left part of it till the morning, and it bred worms and stank. (Exodus 16:16–20)

No matter how much they gathered, they always ended up with the same amount. That is, if they became anxious and thought, *What if the manna is not there for us tomorrow?* and hence they saved some until morning, the extra became spoiled. Once again God is not teaching capitalism; rather, he desires to create a society in which we share with one another while at the same time remain completely dependent on him. This is why the Master tells us to pray, "Give us this day our daily bread."

One would imagine that after just a few weeks of the manna, the Israelites would grow tired of the same old thing every day. Indeed, we read later in the Torah that they did, and that they complained about it as well. It is so difficult for us to find contentment in the simple provision that God gives us—we seem to always be itching for something bigger and better. But from the very inception of Israel's history, their loving heavenly Father always sought to teach them something different: to find peace and solace in what God has provided.

The Shema

The *Shema* is the central creed of the Jewish faith, and in the Gospels Yeshua declared it to be one of the two greatest commandments.[53] It also contains an important lesson for us on the value of generosity. The second line of the *Shema* reads,

> You shall love the LORD your God with all your heart
> and with all your soul and with all your might. (Deuteronomy 6:5)

Loving God has been divided up into three categories: with all one's heart, with all one's soul, and with all one's might. While we ourselves might be inclined to see all three aspects in ethereal, non-tangible forms, the sages break these categories down and explain what each one means:

> "With all your heart" means, with your two impulses, the evil impulse as well as the good impulse; "with all your soul" means, even though he takes your soul [life]; "with all your might" means, with all your money. (m.*Brachot* 9:5)

Loving God with all our heart essentially means loving him with our inclinations, both good ones and bad ones, by curbing them for good.

"Soul" in Hebrew here is the word *nefesh* (נפש), which can mean "life." Loving God with all our soul means loving him even to the point of death or martyrdom.

Yet perhaps one of the most difficult things for us to do is to love God with this third aspect of love: our strength. Here the Hebrew word is *me'od* (מאד), which can mean "strength, property, and wealth." God requires of us that we love him enough even to give up all our worldly possessions. How many of us are really ready to do that? God has not placed us on this earth to store up treasures in this present world but in the World to Come.

We often forget how difficult and devastating this sin of materialism and greed can be. We can learn a valuable lesson from the city of Sodom. It is easy for us to feel good about their destruction when we think that sexual misconduct was the source of their punishment. But let's ask, "What sin really caused Sodom to deserve total destruction?" The Prophet Ezekiel tells us:

> Behold, this was the guilt of your sister Sodom: she and her daughters had pride, excess of food, and prosperous ease, but did not aid the poor and needy. (Ezekiel 16:49)

Sodom's sin was that they were blessed with abundance yet did not share their blessing and bless others in need. Greed and hoarding are serious offenses to which HaShem does not turn a blind eye.

The Mitzvot of Possessions

Besides the *Shema* there are many other mitzvot that teach us about the proper use of our possessions and curb the spirit of greed. For example, the final commandment of the Ten Commandments is "You shall not covet" (Exodus 20:17). Remarkably, it is really the only internal commandment of the ten. Every other commandment can be punished by a court of law, because the transgression of it is both visible and measurable. Yet the sin of coveting goes on in an individual's heart. God places discontent with our lot in life right up there with idolatry and murder.

We have already gone through the numerous tithing commandments of the Torah. All of them guard us against the spirit of covetousness and greed. The Mishnah writes that "tithes form a fence to wealth."[54] It is not that they guard against wealth, but they guard against the dangers that wealth or the desire for wealth can bring, such as greed and materialism. As we pointed out, tithing quickly puts into perspective the fact that all we gain comes from the hand of HaShem.

Yet, as if the tithing system is not enough to persuade us to give, HaShem gives Israel even more mitzvot about generosity. There are many commandments about taking care of the poor and being sensitive to their vulnerable state:

> If you lend money to any of my people with you who is poor, you shall not be like a moneylender to him, and you shall not exact interest from him. If ever you take your neighbor's cloak in pledge, you shall return it to him before the sun goes down, for that is his only covering, and it is his cloak for his body; in what else shall he sleep? And if he cries to me, I will hear, for I am compassionate. (Exodus 22:25–27, emphasis added)

Interestingly enough, the Torah uses the word *'im* (אם) here, which means "if" when speaking about lending money to poor. This seems to imply that the mitzvah to help the poor is optional. Yet in a parallel passage from Deuteronomy, the text states that one is obligated to lend money:

> *You shall* open your hand to him and lend him sufficient for his need, whatever it may be. (Deuteronomy 15:8, emphasis added)

Is this a contradiction? No, the Torah is rather teaching us a lesson that our giving should be both from a sense of obligation and out of free will. The Maharal writes,

> The Torah did not wish the Jew to fulfill this commandment as if he were merely carrying out the decree of the king, but though obligatory, he should carry it out in a spirit of goodwill as a matter of choice, not necessity. (*Gur Aryeh*)[55]

Based on these verses about loaning to the poor and on the fact that an Israelite was forbidden to charge another Israelite interest, Orthodox Jewish groups have set up free loan societies throughout their communities called *gemach* (גמ"ח). Here interest-free loans can be obtained to help individuals get back on their feet after a time of financial difficulty. It causes lending money to be about helping someone out and not about making a profit. The Rambam sees that lending money rather than simply giving it can sometimes be the best form of charity:

> In order to lighten the burden of a poor man one should readily be prepared to lend him aid. This is far more commendable than dispensing charity. In the latter case the needy man's dilemma is obvious and less embarrassing than that of one who has fallen on bad times, and who can be rehabilitated by timely assistance.[56]

Additionally, loans were to be forgiven every seven years with the onset of the *shmittah* (Sabbatical) year. This command tested the hearts of people in the days of the Master, and many chose to skirt their responsibility and not lend money for fear that it would not be paid back. Hillel had to create a legal fiction called *prozebul* (פרוזבול) to help those in desperate need of loans, particularly for farming. This allowed loans that were processed through a court to be free from cancelation even in the seventh year. It was a sad compromise on a sad state of affairs. We can hear a sting of rebuke in Yeshua's words:

> Give to everyone who begs from you, and from one who takes away your goods do not demand them back … If you lend to those from whom you expect to receive, what credit is that to you? Even sinners lend to sinners, to get back the same amount. (Luke 6:30–34)

The Master taught us to pray, "Forgive us our debts, as we also have forgiven our debtors" (Matthew 6:12).

The Torah also stresses over and over that we should be mindful of the most vulnerable of society: the widow and the orphan. Exodus 22:22 states, "You shall not mistreat any widow or fatherless child." James calls this "religion that is pure and undefiled before God."[57] We are warned not to overlook or abuse someone just because he has no one to come to his defense. If we do, it is God who will rise up in his stead and bring justice.

The Torah is chock full of many lessons and commandments that help us guard against materialism and greed. It is from this deep wellspring of Torah knowledge that our Master further instructs on the importance of storing up treasures in heaven.

13
Releasing Our Grip on Materialism

Before we finish our discussion on charity and materialism in the Bible, let's look at a few more parables and sayings from our Master on the subject. Our Rabbi has pin-point precision in showing us the pitfalls of loving the world and has some sound instruction for us on avoiding these traps.

The Parable of the Rich Fool

One of the most illustrative stories on the dangers of greed is the Master's parable of the rich fool:

> He told them a parable, saying, "The land of a rich man produced plentifully, and he thought to himself, 'What shall I do, for I have nowhere to store my crops?' And he said, 'I will do this: I will tear down my barns and build larger ones, and there I will store all my grain and my goods. And I will say to my soul, "Soul, you have ample goods laid up for many years; relax, eat, drink, be merry."' But God said to him, 'Fool! This night your soul is required of you, and the things you have prepared, whose will they be?' So is the one who lays up treasure for himself and is not rich toward God." (Luke 12:15–21)

This man displayed his foolishness by storing up grain that he would in the end never use. He did not understand the principle that God blesses us so that we will in turn bless others. True wealth should be stored up in the kingdom of heaven. Biblical commentator Samuel Tobias Lachs writes, "Wealth given away is wealth stored away; it actually ensures its existence."[58] We hold onto the value of what we are given not by keeping it but by giving it to others for the sake of the kingdom of heaven.

The Master later tells us after finishing the parable, "For where your treasure is, there your heart will be also."[59] When I was in Bible college, a professor once asked me to identify what one thing was on my mind most of the day. "Chances are," the professor said, "this is your god."

Sell Everything?

So where does all this leave us? Should we denounce our property and materialism and give everything to charity? It almost seems as if that is exactly what the Master is saying in Luke 14:33:

> Any one of you who does not renounce all that he has cannot be my disciple.

This is almost identical to what he tells the rich man in Luke 18:22:

> One thing you still lack. Sell all that you have and distribute to the poor, and you will have treasure in heaven; and come, follow me.

Selling everything is an impossible task for most of us. Nor is it asked of us. The disciples in the days of the Master were in a unique situation because Yeshua was present with them. When he called them to follow him as disciples, it was a literal call for them to get up and follow him, taking on full-time careers as students. Unfortunately, we aren't in the same position of having him present.

Likewise, those families that sold their possessions and lived communally in Jerusalem after the resurrection did so because of the presence of the Temple, where they worshiped daily, and the presence of the apostles. That was not the norm for believers in the rest of the world—out in the Diaspora or in Paul's communities.

Poverty for the sake of poverty is not a virtue. We need something to survive on, and many of us have families to feed. Even the apostles knew this. After all, Peter returned to his fishing boats after the death of Yeshua, and Paul had a tent-making business.[60] Obviously they did not rid themselves of all their possessions. There might be a better way to look at these teachings.

Release of the Surplus

The Master was trying to get his disciples to release their grip on material things. Not everyone will be called to give up everything, but we should be able to do so if we are asked. In reality, it appears that the financial call of discipleship is that we are summoned to share of the bounties that God has given us and not hold so tightly to our surplus. It seems that this is what was going on in Jerusalem with the first believers:

> All who believed were together and had all things in common. And they were selling their possessions and belongings and distributing the proceeds to all, as any had need. (Acts 2:44–45)

Rather than being some kind of communal blueprint for a communist society, the idea here is that when there was a need, people would give of their surplus to help with the cause. This conclusion is further solidified in Acts 4:34–35:

> There was not a needy person among them, for as many as were owners of lands or houses sold them and brought the proceeds of what was sold and laid it at the apostles' feet, and it was distributed to each as any had need.

The NIV translates "for as many" as "from time to time" which is the correct sense of the underlying imperfect verb in the Greek. In other words, when a need arose, people would sell what they could, but this does not describe a onetime selling of all a person's possessions. The spirit of Acts is echoed in what the Mishnah describes as the attitude of the pious person. In tractate *Avot* four types of people are described:

> There are four types of people. He who says: "Mine is mine and yours is yours"—this is the average type; and some say, this typifies Sodom; he who says: "Mine is

yours and yours is mine" is an uneducated person; he who says: "Mine is yours and yours is yours" is a pious man; and he who says: "Mine is mine and yours is mine" is a wicked man. (m.*Avot* 9:5)

We should not seek to gain from others but should seek to help others who are in need. Deuteronomy 15:4 stresses that the blessings of the land were given in order to benefit everyone:

There will be no poor among you; for the LORD will bless you in the land that the LORD your God is giving you for an inheritance to possess.

Surely this principle was not meant to enable those who were lazy—we see Paul warning against this attitude in the book of Thessalonians: if one does not work, he should not eat.[61] But it does cause us to realize that there are those who need our help, and we should extend our hand to them in the same way that God has extended his hand to us. The Master tells us that when we hold a banquet, we should invite the poor, the crippled, the lame, and the blind. In times of celebration, we should share the bounty that God has given us to those who suffer lack.

Good Stewards

Let's turn to another of the Master's sayings about righteous and unrighteous wealth:

I tell you, make friends for yourselves by means of unrighteous wealth, so that when it fails they may receive you into the eternal dwellings. One who is faithful in a very little is also faithful in much, and one who is dishonest in a very little is also dishonest in much. If then you have not been faithful in the unrighteous wealth, who will entrust to you the true riches? (Luke 16:9–11)

What is unrighteous wealth? It's not income gained through unrighteous means but, rather, the treasures of earth, whereas the true riches of this statement are the treasures in heaven. Yeshua is saying that if we cannot be faithful with the mundane and material things that he gives us here on earth, how can we be trusted with the true riches of the kingdom?

Being rich is not a sin. Some people get that impression from the story of the rich man and the beggar Lazarus; but remember that Lazarus, the poor man, went to Abraham's bosom, and Abraham, as we read in the Torah, was an exceedingly wealthy man.[62] Nicodemus was also wealthy and yet a faithful disciple of Yeshua.[63] No, God does not condemn wealth; rather, he wants us to be good stewards.

In fact, good stewardship can be seen as a true sign of repentance. For example, consider the story of Zacchaeus:

> Zacchaeus stood and said to the Lord, "Behold, Lord, the half of my goods I give to the poor. And if I have defrauded anyone of anything, I restore it fourfold." And Yeshua said to him, "Today salvation has come to this house, since he also is a son of Abraham." (Luke 19:8–9)

Zacchaeus showed his repentance through action. He attempted to make right the wrong he had done by using his money properly rather than improperly as he had done in the past. Notice that he did not sell everything but only half. This idea of good stewardship is paralleled in the teachings of John the Baptist:

> The crowds asked him, "What then shall we do?" And he answered them, "Whoever has two tunics is to share with him who has none, and whoever has food is to do likewise." (Luke 3:10–11)

Everyone is to apply this teaching differently based upon their own real-life situation, but the principle is the same for all. We must give freely from the surplus that God has provided us with. As the Master tells us, "It is more blessed to give than to receive."[64] This is exactly Paul's point when he teaches the Corinthians about "manna-style" giving. In 2 Corinthians Paul uses the manna story as a springboard for a community of giving:

> If the readiness is there, it is acceptable according to what a person has, not according to what he does not have. For I do not mean that others should be eased and you burdened, but that as a matter of fairness your abundance

at the present time should supply their need, so that their abundance may supply your need, that there may be fairness. As it is written, "Whoever gathered much had nothing left over, and whoever gathered little had no lack [Exodus 16:18]." (2 Corinthians 8:12–15)

Paul's sums it up succinctly—he is calling us to live simply.

The Master calls us to a life of selfless giving. We are not to hold onto the treasures of this world but instead are to have our eyes on the things that really matter. This will look different to different people. Some will indeed be called to give up everything for the sake of the kingdom, while others will be called to give what they can. A good general principle is that we are to give of our surplus—keep what we need, and pass on what we don't.

Yeshua urges us to live simply, always looking out for those who might need our help. But this is a difficult balance. How much should we really give away?

14
The Extent of Charity

From Genesis to Revelation, the Bible is replete with instructions on trusting HaShem for our daily provision. It also contains numerous injunctions urging us to take care of the needy and to provide for those who can't do so for themselves. For the disciple of the Master, charity is not simply a mitzvah of the Torah but rather a way of life. Our lives are to be infused with giving not just of our resources but of ourselves.

Giving until It Hurts

In reality, if our giving doesn't hurt a little, we are not giving enough. A good example of this is the story of when the Master saw the widow giving the mite in Luke 21. The woman in the story did not give a portion of what she had—she gave all that she had. While giving for us might mean that we don't get that cup of coffee or the new book we have been wanting, for her it meant that she might not eat for days. Most of us think that we have it a lot worse than we really do. C.S. Lewis writes,

> Nobody who gets enough food and clothing in a world where most are hungry and cold has any business to talk about "misery." [65]

He continues this theme:

> I do not believe one can settle how much we ought to give. I am afraid the only safe rule is to give more than we can spare. In other words, if our expenditure on comforts, luxuries, amusements, etc., is up to the standard common

among those with the same income as our own, we are probably giving away too little. If our charities do not at all pinch or hamper us, I should say they are too small. There ought to be things we should like to do and cannot do because our charitable expenditures excludes them.[66]

Lewis' words have a real sting of truth to them. Do we give until it hurts, or do we give until it might interfere with our daily priorities? These are questions to ask ourselves daily.

Life of Charity

As we survey the Bible's perspective on charity and materialism, we gain some valuable insights that can help us in the practical application of the laws of tithing. We see that God is constantly impelling his people to put their full trust in him. We see that he calls us to give generously from our surplus, and he calls us to free ourselves from the love of mammon and instead to see the true manna of treasure in heaven. In today's Western society, achieving these principles takes effort and requires us to be constantly on guard against the spirit of materialism. Yet this is nothing less than part of our call to discipleship.

With this background in place, we are now ready to move on to practical application.

15
Tithing in
Modern Christianity

We are nearly to the point at which the rubber meets the road: the practical application of what we have learned about tithing. Let's start by examining how the principle of tithing is carried out both in the contemporary church and, in the next chapter, in Judaism.

Most readers of this book probably grew up in a traditional church setting and are familiar with the age-old Christian practice of setting aside 10 percent of one's income and giving it to the church. Many conservative Christians argue that the tithe must go directly to the church and nowhere else. I certainly remember calculating my income this way even from the time I had my first job as a paper boy. If I had twenty dollars profit in a particular week, I knew that a full two dollars would be going to the offering plate the next Sunday.

Canon Law

Strangely enough, although early churchmen such as Clement of Alexandria, Irenaeus, and Chrysostom stressed the tithing principles, tithing was not fully mandated by the church until about the time of the sixth century, when it became canon law at the Synod of Macon in 585. But as we saw from the story of the Pharisee and the tax-collector, the concept of giving a tithe on all income and not just on agriculture was already present in the days of Yeshua. Also, remember that tithing on everything was practiced by the early Jewish-Christian community as well, as is evidenced in the *Didache*, which seems to command that one tithe on all one's possessions.

How the church maintains the requirement of the tithe today varies. Some say that even though the rest of the Torah's laws were abolished, the laws of tithing in the Torah were never abolished but now apply to one's income. Many feel that pastors function as Christian replacements or extensions of the biblical priests and Levites and therefore the biblical command to give a tithe to the Levites and priests is now transferred to the Christian clergy.

This is a misappropriation of the laws of tithing, because, as we have seen, the biblical tithe pertained to agriculture in the land of Israel. Even if we accept the idea that the tithing commandments now extend to money, this interpretation falls short, because, as we saw, the full weight of the Levitical Torah tithe is over 20 percent and not just 10 percent.

Others argue that while the 10-percent tithe today is not a continuation of the commandments that we find in Exodus, Leviticus, Numbers, and Deuteronomy, it was established in the tithe that Abraham gave to Melchizedek.

The Prosperity Movement

Adherents of the prosperity movement teach that the giving of the tithe is directly proportional to how generously God will financially bless the giver. They cite Malachi 3:11 as evidence:

> Bring the full tithe into the storehouse, that there may be food in my house. And thereby put me to the test, says the LORD of hosts, if I will not open the windows of heaven for you and pour down for you a blessing until there is no more need.

According to the prosperity teachers, if we tithe, we will be blessed; if we do not, we will be cursed. Some even teach that if a person suffers financial hardships, it is due to a lack of tithing. As we discovered, however, the passages that this theology is based upon are taken completely out of context.

Yet despite the emphasis on tithing in the church today, actual observance of the practice is at an all-time low. A study made in

2002 by the Barna Group throughout the United States showed that only 3 percent of adults contributed 10 percent of their income to churches, while the number of adults who called themselves born-again Christians and tithed was at about 6 percent. Institutional loyalty runs thin nowadays, even when that institution is the church. Many Christians question whether or not the tithe is biblically obligatory.

So let's ask the question: does the church really have a right to say that tithing 10 percent is a biblical requirement? Before we fully answer this question, we need to examine the Jewish practice of the tithe today.

16
Tithing in Modern Judaism

J udaism still sees the Torah's commandments of tithing as binding and in force, but not all the commandments can be practically applied today. For example, without a Temple there are no sacrifices today. Tithing somewhat falls into the same category. The Torah specifically stipulates that tithes are on agriculture and that most of them are applicable only within the land of Israel. In addition to that, many of the tithes are Temple-dependent, and we find that very few of the tithing commandments can be observed in the land of Israel, much less outside it.

Practically speaking, Judaism does not spiritualize these mitzvot nor transfer them as Christianity does. For example, Judaism does not regard the modern-day rabbi as a replacement for the priest or Levite and therefore deserving of tithes. As a result, very few of the biblical tithing commandments are literally applicable for the average person. In fact, almost none.

Ten Percent

It may come as a surprise to some that, just as in Christianity, Judaism teaches that setting aside a 10-percent tithe of all income is the normal practice and an expected spiritual discipline for those who call themselves Torah observant. In Hebrew this is called *ma'aser kesafim* ("tithing on money," מעשר כספים). As has been pointed out more than once, this goes all the way back to the Second Temple period in which it had become the practice of some to tithe on all their income and not just on agriculture. We find evidence of this in the Gospels as well as in extra-biblical literature.

In fact, Judaism teaches that giving a 10-percent tithe on one's income has always been the norm and is assumed by the Torah. The logic is simple. The Torah assumes that everyone is to set aside 10 percent of their income for the LORD, just as Abraham and Jacob did. Whenever God blessed a person with something, he was to give a tithe of it back to the LORD.

The whole culture of the ancient Near East practiced some form of tithing. The Torah never included a law that said, "Thou shalt set aside 10 percent for the LORD." Instead, it includes laws explaining how to set aside the tithes on agriculture grown in the land of Israel. Why does agriculture in the land of Israel need special laws? Because the land does not belong to the Israelites, it belongs to God. The people of Israel were more like sharecroppers than landowners. That's why special laws of tithing applied to agriculture in the land of Israel.

If a person wasn't a farmer, however, he could assume a flat tithe of 10 percent. For example, if a man was a potter and made pots and sold them, he would simply tithe 10 percent of the profit he made as a potter—giving it to the Levites, the priesthood, the Temple, or maybe even to the poor and needy—or perhaps using some of it to purchase animals to sacrifice at the festivals, as it says in the Torah:

> Three times a year all your males shall appear before the LORD your God at the place that he will choose: at the Feast of Unleavened Bread, at the Feast of Weeks, and at the Feast of Booths. They shall not appear before the LORD empty-handed. (Deuteronomy 16:16)

The 10-percent tithe is the baseline. Higher minimums apply to agriculture practiced on the soil of God's holy land.

We noted from an early midrash on Deuteronomy 14:22, "You shall tithe all the yield of your seed that comes from the field year by year," that the word "all" was interpreted as redundant and therefore the verse taken to mean that we are required to give a tenth on all forms of income.

Tithe for the Poor

There are others who teach that the tithe of a flat 10 percent on our income is not based on agricultural tithing commandments but is rather a minimum amount to be set aside to give to the poor. This would be considered in fulfillment of verses such as Deuteronomy 15:7–8:

> If among you, one of your brothers should become poor, in any of your towns within your land that the LORD your God is giving you, you shall not harden your heart or shut your hand against your poor brother, but you shall open your hand to him and lend him sufficient for his need, whatever it may be.

There is even a statement in the *Jerusalem Talmud* to back this up that states, "In Usha they voted that a person should set aside a fifth of his property to carry out a mitzvah [of charity]."[67] Obviously, one fifth is more than a 10-percent tithe. One fifth is 20 percent. By separating a substantial tithe for the purpose of providing for the poor, it was certain that a person would fulfill the mitzvah of charity and have money to give whenever the need arose.

A General Rule

The overarching rule in Judaism today is that one set aside at least a tenth of one's income for charity. The rabbis, however, set a maximum of 20 percent lest one give away too much and become dependent on charity himself. As with most things in halachah, there are debates as to the specifics and levels of obligation, but 10 percent is the general practice.

However, in Judaism the tithe does not go only to the local synagogue. Unlike general Christian practice, there is not an opinion that the full tithe should be given to one's home congregation. Instead, the tithe is spent primarily on charity for the poor. According to some opinions it can also be used, under certain circumstances, for purchasing Torah books for community use, paying for certain essential ceremonial expenses, and other things as needs arise. For the most part, though, it is intended for the poor. There are also special halachic rulings to aid those who simply cannot afford to give 10 percent.

The Chofetz Chaim, a prominent rabbi in Jewish thought, teaches that the tithe can be used to support needy members of one's extended family or the poor of the local community. When there are no immediate needs like this, the tithe should be given to those who dedicate their time to learning and teaching Torah. The original principle of tithing to the priesthood and Levites reflects this idea. Those whose time is devoted to serving HaShem sincerely are the rightful recipients of the people's tithes, and God promises to bless those who support his servants. Nonetheless, the poor take precedence.

Now that we have surveyed the practice of tithing in both Judaism and Christianity, we can begin to discuss what practical application of tithing might look like for Messianic believers today.

17
Obligation or Principle?

At First Fruits of Zion, we believe that all of God's Torah is perpetual and that, as our Master says, not one jot or tittle of it will pass away until all is accomplished. It goes without saying then that the laws of tithing that we outlined in earlier chapters are still applicable, as much as they can be without a Temple. That is to say that if the Temple were rebuilt and the priesthood reinstated, all the Bible's laws on tithing would immediately go into full effect for all farmers in the land of Israel.

But what about the principle of tithing 10 percent of our incomes?

A Biblical Principle

So we ask the question again: as believers in Messiah, are we obligated to tithe today? The answer is yes and no. While we should hesitate to make tithing a biblical commandment and a strict obligation, there is ample evidence from the Bible, from history, and from both Jewish and Christian tradition that tithing is a biblical principle.

We should give at least 10 percent of our income to the kingdom, sharing it with those who are in need and with those who teach us the Word of God.

Judaism and Christianity rarely agree on anything, but they unanimously regard giving 10 percent of one's income to the LORD's work as a serious obligation for godly living. We would be fools to ignore that, especially in today's world.

We need to remember that those of us who live today in first-world nations like the United States are the most obscenely wealthy people with the highest standard of living in all human history. If previous generations who lived—by comparison to us—in poverty and squalor faithfully gave 10 percent, then who are we to exempt ourselves from this simple minimum?

For biblical support we need look no further than the two stories of Abraham and Jacob tithing that we have already examined. Each patriarch offered up a tithe as an offering of praise and thanks to HaShem for his circumstances—Abraham for the victory he had just won in battle and Jacob for the future fulfillment of the promises that God had made to him. In both cases the principle that is established is not just giving something but giving a tenth.

We have many commandments in the Torah about providing for the poor and needy, and we also have the biblical example in the Torah of providing for the priests and Levites with tithes. HaShem told the priests and Levites that they were to have no inheritance in the land. Instead, he was their inheritance. This means that they had no income from a secular vocation—they worked full time ministering to the community, ministering in the Word of God, and carrying out their sacred duties.

While it would be careless of us to allegorize the Torah's commandments on tithing to the Levites and apply that to pastors and Bible teachers today, nevertheless, as in the patriarchal stories, a principle is established in them. From these commands we learn a principle of supporting those who do the work of the kingdom.

The Laborer Deserves His Food

This is a principle that our Master taught. He told his disciples to accept community support. He said, "The laborer deserves his food."[68]

Additionally, Paul argued that as an apostle, he was worthy of community support, and he considered the fact that he provided for himself as something exceptional, not normal. Moreover, he required all his communities to pay a tithe-like tribute to the mother church in Jerusalem—the congregation of James, the brother of the Master, and of the apostles. For example, Paul took up a collection from the church in Corinth:

On the first day of every week, each of you is to put something aside and store it up, as he may prosper, so that there will be no collecting when I come. And when I arrive, I will send those whom you accredit by letter to carry your gift to Jerusalem. (1 Corinthians 16:2–3)

This offering was then given to believers in Jerusalem, where the leadership for the Messianic community was. Although Paul here says nothing about 10 percent or tithing, it is as if he was taking the principle of providing for the Temple given in the Torah and using it to provide for the Jewish community, which included the Jerusalem Council leadership, a sort of spiritual Temple.

Paul, in fact, makes it abundantly clear that teachers should be provided for:

Let the elders who rule well be considered worthy of double honor, especially those who labor in preaching and teaching. For the Scripture says, "You shall not muzzle an ox when it treads out the grain," and, "The laborer deserves his wages." (1 Timothy 5:17–18)

Those who are assuming priestly and Levitical-type roles are to be taken care of.

Judaism and Christianity Agree

The fact that both Christianity and Judaism feel that tithing is important should give us pause. Both religions are steeped in traditions thousands of years old, and both regard the practice of tithing as a necessary and important part of a godly walk. When we examine the Christian perspective and the Jewish perspective, we can see that each offers its own merits.

Christianity stresses providing for teachers, congregational leaders, and community expenses with the tithe. As we have seen, this thinking was present as far back as the first century in which, the *Didache* tells us, a tithe of sorts was given to the prophets, who were the teachers.

Jewish tradition provides for us an example of taking care of the poor by tithing. (In Judaism, many of the poor are the Torah teachers, the rabbis, and the scholars, so Judaism supports its teachers and pastors too.) Judaism established a 10-percent minimum because it recognized the biblical precedent for this in the Torah itself, and also they knew that if no minimum was established, many would not give anything at all. It is a sad state of humanity but, at the same time, a very true reality. By specifically setting aside this money and separating it before anything else is spent, it becomes available to help others in need without the worry of tapping into one's budget.

Supporting Your Community

When we speak of the importance of tithing it is important to point out that, biblically, no one such as a church or congregation has the authority to claim that they deserve your full tithe. One is free to distribute this tithe how one wishes to ministries and charities. At the same time, it stands to reason that if you are being spiritually fed at a particular congregation and participating in that community, and that the community also gives to the needy and does social work and supports missions outreach, why not give them the money rather than looking for causes to help on your own? Many congregations distribute their money between salaries and internal ministry groups that do everything from running food banks and soup kitchens to supporting missions overseas.

You might belong to a church where the standard is to give 10 percent directly to the church. There is nothing wrong with that, so long as that church is doing the work of the kingdom. Ultimately, where you do decide to give your tithe is between you and God, but the most important point is that we are giving.

Summary

As I stated at the outset, we should be hesitant to set the require-ment of a 10 percent tithe as a biblical injunction or demand, but there is much biblical and historical evidence that points to the validity of the practice of tithing. Yet, even when we do give a percent tithe it does not automatically free us from the spirit of mammon. We should consider 10 percent as a minimum, but don't forget the rich young man. Our Master told him to sell all that he had and give it all to the poor. Obviously, we can't all be Saint Francis of Assisi, but many of us can give much more than 10 percent.

Ten percent is not some magical number that takes materialism and greed out of our lives. Yes, for some 10 percent will be tough to give, but for others it's just a drop in the bucket. Your own conscience will have to direct you on this, but remember the wise saying of John Bunyan: "There was a man, some called him mad; The more he gave, the more he had." This logic goes against the worldly flow but it is right in line with the biblical flow.

Tithing is a great way to bless and provide for the needs of others but, as we have learned, giving in the biblical sense is not limited to tithing.

18
Charity beyond Tithing

We must remember that there are many other ways we can give charity besides merely from our tithe. Here are a couple of practical examples.

Free Loan Society

In an earlier chapter we briefly covered the idea of the free loan society. As you remember, the Torah tells the Israelites that they are not allowed to charge interest to one another. Therefore, in Jewish communities today it is common to set up societies to which people in need can go and procure interest-free loans. By this method an individual can get the loan he needs without the stress of having to take years and years to pay it off due to high interest rates. In Judaism this is considered one of the highest forms of charity, because it allows people a sense of dignity. Although they receive immediate help, it becomes their responsibility to work hard to pay it back.

While for most of us loaning out a high dollar amount to someone in need of financial help might not be realistic, perhaps you could be instrumental in setting up a free loan society at your church or synagogue. Craig Blomberg, in his book *Neither Poverty nor Riches*, tells of a church that has implemented a unique twist on this. He writes,

> A church in Seattle decided to raise funds so that young first-time home buyers could pay cash outright for their property. These Christians then contracted to pay back

the church what their mortgage payments would have been to fund further ministry and create more home-buying opportunities for other church members. When one considers that the average Westerner spends more on paying a home mortgage (principle plus interest) than on any other single lifetime expenditure, it is tragic that more Christians are not seeking to replicate this model.[69]

Here, although the loans are not interest free, the money that would have gone to interest actually goes straight to charity. The sky's the limit on ideas, but it takes *us* to go out and create something.

Tzedakah Box

Another idea could be something as simple as buying a *tzedakah* ("charity," צדקה) box from a local Judaica shop. They come in all different shapes, sizes, and colors to fit all kinds of tastes. Put this somewhere prominent in your house. Every time you have loose change or find a coin on the ground, put it in the box. Maybe even skip that cup of coffee from the coffee shop one day and put the money you would have spent in the charity box instead. It may seem like a small thing, but over time these funds can add up.

When the box is full, you get to decide where it goes. Maybe a needy neighbor down the street could use a full tank of gas, or perhaps you can give it to your favorite overseas charity that provides food and clothing for those in the third world. The possibilities are endless.

Listening for Opportunities

Every time poverty statistics appear on the news, we are shocked. We hear that two in five or one in three are living below the poverty line. We can't imagine who these people could be, because everyone around us looks as if they are doing fine.

Finding those in need sometimes requires us to be attentive and listen. How many times a day does someone cryptically allude to a need while we are too busy to really listen? In our day and age, with technology like the Internet and e-mail, we have opportunities as never before to help people. When we discover a need, we can communicate with multiple people in multiple ways to help.

Yet sometimes what means the most to others is when we quietly meet someone's need in a special way. When we take time to listen to someone, we can often obtain details that can help us be quite specific in how we aid the person. In a world that is moving faster than ever before, in which people seem to have little time for meaningful conversation, listening can indicate to a needy person how much we care for them and their friendship.

If we want to help people, all we have to do is open our eyes and ears as we remember the words of our Master: "For you always have the poor with you."[70]

Conclusion

If each one of us takes a good look at our lives, we can see that God has blessed us in many ways. It is our biblical injunction to share this blessing with others. Those of us living in Western society have been provided with much abundance. Tithing becomes one of our main vehicles for not only supporting our congregations, teachers, and ministries but for sharing with others what God has so graciously given us.

As we have seen, 10 percent should be seen as a minimum and not a maximum. The tithe is a good number to keep us in check, but it should not be looked at as a checkmark that will eliminate the spirit of mammon from inside us.

In closing, hear the wisdom of Solomon:

> Two things I ask of you; deny them not to me before I die: Remove far from me falsehood and lying; give me neither poverty nor riches; feed me with the food that is needful for me, lest I be full and deny you and say, "Who is the LORD?" or lest I be poor and steal and profane the name of my God. (Proverbs 30:7–9)

May grace and peace be multiplied to you in the knowledge of God and of Yeshua our Master.[71] Amen and amen.

Endnotes

1   Moshe Weinfeld, "Tithe," *Encyclopedia Judaica* (2nd ed.): 19:736.

2   Genesis 47:24.

3   Weinfeld, "Tithe," 19:736.

4   Weinfeld, "Tithe," 19:736.

5   Weinfeld, "Tithe," 19:737.

6   The Ramban saw this as foreshadowing the tithes that Israel would later be required to give to the priesthood.

7   Ezekiel 16:49.

8   According to rabbinic tradition Isaac tithed as well (*Pirkei deRabbi Eli'ezer* 33).

9   E.g., Numbers 18:12; Deuteronomy 18:4. See Rabbi Nosson Scherman and Rabbi Meir Zlotowitz, ed., *The Artscroll Mishnah Series: Seder Zeraim Volume IV(b): Maasros/Maaser Sheni* (Brooklyn, NY: Mesorah Publications, 2003), 5.

10   Rabbi Yisrael Meir HaKohen, *The Concise Book of Mitzvoth: The Commandments Which Can Be Observed Today* (New York, NY: Feldheim, 1990), 291–293.

11   There is, however, an interesting tradition that Noah practiced some of the tithing mitzvot: "For three years the fruit of everything that is eaten will not be gathered: and in the fourth year its fruit will be accounted holy [and they will offer the first-fruits], acceptable before the Most High God, who created heaven and earth and all things. Let them offer in abundance the first of the wine and oil [as] first-fruits on the altar of the Lord, who receives it, and what is left let the servants of the house of the Lord eat before the altar which receives [it]. And in the fifth year make ye the release so that ye release it in righteousness and uprightness, and ye shall be righteous, and all that you plant shall prosper" (*Jubilees* 7:36–37).

12   For this section I have relied upon Rabbi Shaul Reichenberg, ed., *The Procedure for Setting Aside T'rumot and Ma'asrot* (Aharon Angstreich, trans.; New York, NY: Feldheim, 1991).

13   "By Torah law it is in effect only in the land of Israel … And so too, by the Sages' ruling, it is equally in effect in various locations in the regions close to the Land" (HaKohen, *The Concise Book of Mitzvoth*, 285).

14   "By the law of the Torah, this applies [only] to grain, wine, and oil, although some say to all produce; but by law of the Sages it applies to all food that is stored, which was grown from the soil" (HaKohen, *The Concise Book of Mitzvoth*, 285).

15   y.*Bikkurim* 3:1. See also m.*Pe'ah* 1:1.

16   m.*Bikkurim* 1:6.

17   m.*Bikkurim* 3.

18   "It is in force when the Temple is extant, for men, and in regard to the produce of the land of Israel, Syria and Transjordan, but not in regard to produce outside the land" (Rabbi Aaron HaLevi, *Séfer haḤinnuch: The Book of [Mitzvah] Education* [5 vols.; New York, NY: Feldheim, 1991], 1:349).

19   m.*Pe'ah* 1:1–2.

20   m.*Pe'ah* 7:3–4.

21   See m.*Pe'ah* 4.

22   "By law of the Torah, this is in effect in the Land [of Israel]; and by law of the Sages, outside the Land [in other countries as well]. But some hold that this means specifically the regions near the land, where there is the obligation of *trumah* and the tithe by the law of the Sages" (HaKohen, *The Concise Book of Mitzvoth*, 279).

23   For additional territories surrounding the land of Israel in which work in the field is also considered forbidden in the *Shmittah* year, see HaLevi, *Séfer haḤinnuch*, 1:331–333.

24   D. T. Lancaster, *Torah Club: Depths of the Torah* (Marshfield, MO: First Fruits of Zion, 2013), 1042–1043.

25   HaKohen, *The Concise Book of Mitzvoth*, 71.

26   HaKohen, *The Concise Book of Mitzvoth*, 69–71.

27   HaKohen, *The Concise Book of Mitzvoth*, 69–71.

28   HaLevi, *Séfer haḤinnuch*, 3:507–513.

29   m.*Shekalim* 1:1–2.

30   HaLevi, *Séfer haḤinnuch*, 1:399.

31   Rabbi Samson Raphael Hirsch, *Horeb: A Philosophy of Jewish Laws and Observances* (trans. Isidore Grunfeld; London, England: Soncino, 2002), 196.

32   John Lightfoot, *A Commentary on the New Testament from the Talmud and Hebraica* (4 vols.; Peabody, MA: Hendrickson, 2003), 3:185.

33 *Didache* 13:7.

34 *Sifrei* to Deuteronomy 14:22 as quoted in *Tosafot Ta'anit* 9a as translated in Cyril Domb, ed., *Maaser Kesafim: Giving a Tenth to Charity* (New York, NY: Feldheim, 1982), 20.

35 m.*Ma'aserot* 4:5; m.*Shevi'it* 7:1; m.*Demai* 2:1.

36 David Instone-Brewer, *Traditions of the Rabbis from the Era of the New Testament*, vol. 1: *Prayer and Agriculture* (Grand Rapids, MI: Eerdmans, 2004), 182.

37 Randall Buth and Brian Kvasnica, "Temple Authorities and Tithe Evasion: The Linguistic Background and Impact of the Parable of the Vineyard, the Tenants and the Son" in *Jesus' Last Week: Jerusalem Studies in the Synoptic Gospels*, vol. 1 (R. Steven Notley, Marc Turnage, and Brian Becker, eds.; Boston, MA: Brill, 2006), 53–80.

38 Reuven Hammer, *Sifre: A Tannaitic Commentary on the Book of Deuteronomy* (New Haven, CT: Yale University Press, 1986), 152. See also b.*Bava Metzia* 88a; y.*Pe'ah* 1:5.

39 Hammer, *Sifre*, 434.

40 Buth and Kvasnica, "Temple Authorities and Tithe Evasion" in *Jesus' Last Week*, 68.

41 Mark D. Nanos, *The Mystery of Romans: The Jewish Context of Paul's Letter* (Minneapolis, MN: Fortress, 1996), 308–320.

42 Exodus 2:4; Numbers 12:15.

43 Exodus 13:19; Deuteronomy 34:6.

44 Exodus 1:22, 14:28.

45 D. T. Lancaster, *Torah Club: Voice of the Prophets* (Marshfield, MO: First Fruits of Zion, 2009), C8.

46 The *Didache* even advocates a form of this mitzvah to be observed by Gentile believers in the Diaspora: "When you make a batch of bread dough, take the first part and give it according to the commandment" (13:5).

47 Huub van de Sandt and David Flusser, *The Didache: Its Jewish Sources and its Place in Early Judaism and Christianity* (Minneapolis, MN: Fortress, 2002), 361–362.

48 D. T. Lancaster, *Torah Club: Unrolling the Scroll* (Marshfield, MO: First Fruits of Zion, 2007), 598.

49 Samuel Tobias Lachs, *A Rabbinic Commentary on the New Testament: The Gospels of Matthew, Mark and Luke* (Hoboken, NJ: KTAV, 1987), 129–130.

50 Wayne Martindale and Jerry Root, *The Quotable Lewis* (Carol Stream, IL: Tyndale, 1990), 118.

51   Craig L. Blomberg, *Neither Poverty nor Riches: A Biblical Theology of Possessions* (Leicester, England: InterVarsity Press, 1999), 132.

52   Blomberg, *Neither Poverty nor Riches*, 21.

53   Mark 12:29–30.

54   m.*Avot* 3:17.

55   Translation from Nehama Liebowitz, *New Studies in Shemot*, vol. 2 (Jerusalem, Israel: World Zionist Organization, 1986), 407.

56   Translation from Liebowitz, *New Studies in Shemot*, vol. 2, 407.

57   James 1:27.

58   Lachs, *A Rabbinic Commentary on the New Testament*, 126.

59   Matthew 6:21.

60   John 21:3; Acts 18:3.

61   2 Thessalonians 3:10.

62   Luke 16:20–31; Genesis 13:2.

63   b.*Gittin* 56a.

64   Acts 20:35.

65   Martindale and Root, *The Quotable Lewis*, 118.

66   Martindale and Root, *The Quotable Lewis*, 245.

67   y.*Pe'ah* 1:1.

68   Matthew 10:10.

69   Blomberg, *Neither Poverty nor Riches*, 250–251.

70   Matthew 26:11; Mark 14:7. See also John 12:8.

71   2 Peter 1:2.

Appendix 1
Tithe Chart

Name	Torah Reference	Quantity	According to Torah when the Temple stands	According to halachah without a Temple
Ma'aser Rishon ("first tithe")	Numbers 18:24	A tenth	Given to Levite	Kept by owner or given to Levite
Trumat Ma'aser ("offering tithe")	Numbers 18:26	A tenth of the *ma'aser rishon*	Given to priest	Buried
Ma'aser Sheni ("second tithe")	Deuteronomy 14:22	A tenth of what is left in years 1, 2, 4, and 5	Eaten in Jerusalem in a pilgrimage	Redeemed
Ma'aser Ani ("poor tithe")	Deuteronomy 14:28	A tenth of what is left in years 3 and 6	Given to the poor	Given to the poor

* Based in part on Rabbi Reichenberg, *The Procedure for Setting Aside T'rumot and Ma'asrot*, 11.